"With the empathy of a therapist and the authority of a linguistics professor, Tannen stretches her scholarship further onward.... In her trademark clear, well-organized style, and generously using examples from her own life, Tannen moves from arena to arena, backing her thesis with plenty of research."
—*Entertainment Weekly*

I Only Say This Because I Love You:
Talking to Your Parents, Partner, Sibs, and Kids
When You're All Adults

"Tannen's great gift, and the one that makes this book so worthwhile, is the clarity she offers for emotionally charged familial situations.... She guides the reader to listen in a new and responsive way."
—Wendy Wasserstein, *Washington Post Book World*

"Impressive, eminently useful insights. . . . One seemingly modest but potentially life-changing gift we can give [our families] is to try out Tannen's style of careful, good-humored attention to the ways talking connects us." —*Salon*

You're Wearing THAT?
Understanding Mothers and Daughters in Conversation

"Deborah Tannen decodes the veiled insults, *hmms*, and *oh, reallys?* between mothers and daughters. The implications behind the spoken words are so familiar, it hurts when you laugh."
—*O, The Oprah Magazine*

"The effect of [Tannen's] anecdotes and analysis is to reassure her readers that they are not alone."
—*Wall Street Journal*

You Were Always Mom's Favorite!
Sisters in Conversation Throughout Their Lives

"Tannen, renowned sociologist of conversation, studies one of the most intense and burdened relations of all: that between sisters. 'Love/hate' doesn't begin to describe the elation and heartbreak, the humor and perplexed contradictions revealed in this delightful book." —*Philadelphia Inquirer*

"If you have a sister, you will probably recognize every detail and laugh or cry; if not, it will fill you in on everything you suspected about these potent and thorny relationships. . . . Tannen's deeply personal new work deals with what she considers life's most influential bond and the often unyielding competition always lurking just below the surface." —*The Daily Beast*

About the Author

DEBORAH TANNEN is University Professor and professor of linguistics at Georgetown University. Among her many books, *You Just Don't Understand: Women and Men in Conversation* was on the *New York Times* bestseller list for nearly four years, including eight months as number 1, and it has been translated into thirty languages. *You're Wearing THAT?: Understanding Mothers and Daughters in Conversation* and *You Were Always Mom's Favorite!: Sisters in Conversation Throughout Their Lives* were also *New York Times* bestsellers; *Talking from 9 to 5: Women and Men at Work* was a *New York Times* business bestseller; *The Argument Culture: Stopping America's War of Words* won the Common Ground Book Award; and *I Only Say This Because I Love You: Talking to Your Parents, Partner, Sibs, and Kids When You're All Adults* won the Books for a Better Life Award.

Tannen has written for and been featured in most major magazines and newspapers, including the *New York Times, Washington Post, USA Today, Time, Newsweek,* and *Harvard Business Review.* She is a frequent guest on television and radio news and information shows, including *The Colbert Report, 20/20,* the *Today* show, *Good Morning America, The Oprah Winfrey Show,* and NPR's *Morning Edition, All Things Considered,* and *Diane Rehm Show.*

She also has been McGraw Distinguished Lecturer at Princeton University and was a fellow at the Center for Advanced Study in the Behavioral Sciences, following a term in residence at the Institute for Advanced Study in Princeton, New Jersey. In addition to her books and articles about language in personal and public life, she also has published poems, short stories, and essays. Her play *An Act of Devotion* is included in *The Best American Short Plays: 1993–1994*. It was produced, together with her play *Sisters*, by Horizons Theater.

www.deborahtannen.com

That's *Not* What I Meant!

Also by Deborah Tannen

You Were Always Mom's Favorite!
Sisters in Conversation Throughout Their Lives

You're Wearing THAT?
Understanding Mothers and Daughters in Conversation

I Only Say This Because I Love You:
Talking to Your Parents, Partner, Sibs,
and Kids When You're All Adults

The Argument Culture:
Stopping America's War of Words

Talking from 9 to 5:
Women and Men at Work

You Just Don't Understand:
Women and Men in Conversation

That's *Not* What I Meant!

How Conversational Style Makes
or Breaks Relationships

DEBORAH TANNEN

HARPER

NEW YORK · LONDON · TORONTO · SYDNEY

HARPER

Grateful acknowledgment is made for permission to reprint the following: "Stars, Fish," copyright © 1983 by Nancy Schoenberger. Originally appeared in *The American Poetry Review*, vol. 11, no. 3. "Killing Me Softly," copyright © 1972 by Charles Fox and Norman Gimble. All rights reserved. Excerpts from *Grown Ups*, copyright © Jules Feiffer. Used by permission of the Lantz Company.

A hardcover edition of this book was published in 1986 by William Morrow and Company, Inc.

FIRST HARPER PAPERBACK PUBLISHED 2011.

Library of Congress Cataloging-in-Publication Data is available upon request.

ISBN 978-0-06-206299-4 (Harper paperback)

18 19 20 LSC 20 19 18 17 16 15 14 13 12 11

To my teachers in linguistics:

A. L. Becker
Wallace L. Chafe
John J. Gumperz
Robin Tolmach Lakoff

who selflessly gave me the insights of their work to form the foundation of mine, even as they encouraged me to do my own work and to write and talk about it in my own voice, both within and beyond the bounds of academia

Preface

A student who took the course on cross-cultural communication that I teach in the Linguistics Department at Georgetown University commented that the course saved her marriage. At scholarly meetings, my fellow linguists stop me in the hall to tell me that they showed one of my articles to friends or relatives, and it saved their marriages.

What can linguistics have to do with saving marriages? Linguistics is the academic discipline devoted to understanding how language works. Relationships are made, maintained, and broken through talk, so linguistics provides a concrete way of understanding how relationships are made, maintained, and broken. There are branches of linguistics that are concerned mainly with the history or the grammar or the symbolic representation of language. But there are also branches of the field—sociolinguistics, discourse analysis, and anthropological linguistics—that are concerned with understanding how people use language in their everyday lives, and how people from different cultures use language in different ways. This book grows out of these branches of linguistics.

But the student who said my course saved her marriage and her husband are both American. What does cross-cultural communication have to do with them? It has to do with everyone, because all communication is more or less cross-cultural. We learn to use language as we grow up, and growing up in different parts of the country, having different ethnic, religious, or class backgrounds, even just being male or female—all result in different ways of talking, which I call conversational style. And subtle differences in conversational style result in individually minor but cumulatively overwhelming misunderstandings and disappointments.

As the novelist E. M. Forster put it in *A Passage to India*, "a pause in the wrong place, an intonation misunderstood, and a whole conversation went awry." When conversations go awry, we look for causes, and usually find them by blaming others or ourselves. The most generous-minded among us blame the relationship. This book shows how much of this blame is misplaced. Bad feelings are often the result of misunderstandings that arise from differences in conversational style.

A talk-show host once introduced me by saying that in his long career he had read many books about speaking, but they were all about public speaking. Yet most of the talk we engage in during our lives is not public but private speaking: talk between two or among a few people. This book is about private speaking: how it works, why it goes well sometimes and badly at other times. It explains the invisible processes of conversational style that shape relationships. Understanding these processes restores a sense of control over our lives, making it possible to improve communication and relationships in all the settings in which people talk to each other: at work, in interviews, in public affairs, and most important of all, at home.

Acknowledgments

Now is the time to thank those who have believed in and supported me: my agent, Rhoda Weyr, my editor, Maria Guarnaschelli, Amy Gross of *Vogue* magazine, my parents, Dorothy and Eli Tannen, my sisters, Naomi and Mimi Tannen, my friends Karl Goldstein, June McKay, Lucy Ray, and David Wise. I am especially grateful to those who read early drafts and gave me critical comments: A. L. Becker, Naomi Tannen, and David Wise.

Nearly everyone I encounter becomes a potential source of examples. My family, friends, students, and colleagues, and also unnamed members of audiences and callers to talk shows on which I've appeared, have all generously offered their own experiences, which have helped me understand conversation and illustrate that understanding for others. Many of these have to go unnamed (but are hereby thanked). Some of those whose names I know are: Tom Anselmo, Tom Brazaitis, Mark Clarke, Sysse Engberg, Ralph Fasold, Crawford Feagin, Thaisa Frank, Jo Ann Goldberg, Karl Goldstein, Paul Goldstein, Walter Gorman, Donald Wei Hsiung,

Acknowledgments

Imelda Idar, Deborah Lange, Bill Layher, Joyce Muis-Lowery, Susie Napper, Carol Newman, Mathilde Paterakis, Marcia Perlstein, Eileen Price, David Rabin, Laurel Hadassah Rabin, Lucy Ray, Dan Read, Chuck Richardson, Cynthia Roy, Debby Schiffrin, Ron Scollon, Naomi Tannen, Jackie Tanner, Anne Walker, and David Wye. My thanks to them, and to those who have found their way into my examples through no act of will, but simply by interacting with me.

Contents

Contents

I.

Linguistics and Conversational Style

CHAPTER ONE

The Problem Is the Process

You know the feeling: You meet someone for the first time, and it's as if you've known each other all your lives. Everything goes smoothly. You know just what she means; she knows just what you mean. You laugh at the same time. Your sentences and hers have a perfect rhythm. You feel terrific; you're doing everything right. And you think she's terrific too.

But you also know the other feeling: You meet someone, you try to be friendly, to make a good impression, but everything goes wrong. There are uncomfortable silences. You fish for topics. You bump into each other as you both start at once and then both stop. You start to say something interesting but he cuts you off. He starts saying something and never seems to finish. You try to lighten the mood and he looks as if you punched him in the stomach. He says what may be intended as a joke but is more rude than funny. Whatever you do to make things better makes them worse.

If conversation always followed the first pattern, I wouldn't have to write this book. If it always followed the second, no one would ever talk to anyone else and nothing would get done. Talk is mostly somewhere in the middle. We do get things done; we talk to family and friends and colleagues and neighbors. Sometimes what people say seems to make perfect sense; sometimes it sounds a little odd. If someone doesn't quite get our point, we let it go, the talk continues, and no one pays much attention.

But if an important outcome hangs on the conversation—if it's a job interview, a business meeting, or a doctor's appointment—the results can be very serious. If it's a public negotiation or an international summit conference, the results can be dire indeed. And if the conversation is with the most important person in your life, the little hitches can become big ones, and you can end up in a conversation of the second sort without knowing how you got there. If this happens all the time—at home, at work, or in routine day-to-day encounters, so that you feel misunderstood all the time and never quite understand what others are getting at—you start to doubt your own ability, or even your sanity. Then you can't not pay attention.

For example, Judy Scott is applying for a job as office manager at the headquarters of an ice-cream distributor—a position she's well qualified for. Her last job, although it was called "administrative assistant," actually involved running the whole office, and she did a great job. But at the interview, she never gets a chance to explain this. The interviewer does all the talking, Judy leaves feeling frustrated—and she doesn't get the job.

Or at home: Sandy and Matt have a good marriage. They love each other and are quite happy. But a recurring source of tension is that Sandy often feels that Matt doesn't really listen to her. He asks her a question, but before she can answer, he asks another—or starts to answer it himself. When they get together with Matt's friends, the conversation goes so fast, Sandy can't get a word in edgewise. Afterward, Matt complains that she was too quiet, though she certainly isn't quiet when she gets together with *her* friends. Matt thinks it's because she doesn't like his friends, but the only reason Sandy doesn't like them is that she feels they ignore her—and she can't find a way to get into their conversation.

Sometimes strains in a conversation reflect real differences between people: they *are* angry at each other; they really are at cross-purposes. Books have been written about this situation: how to fight fair, how to assert yourself. But sometimes strains and kinks develop when there really are no basic differences of opinion, when everyone is sincerely trying to get along. This is the type of miscommunication that drives people crazy. And it is usually caused by differences in conversational style.

A perfectly tuned conversation is a vision of sanity—a ratification of one's way of being human and one's place in the world. And nothing is more deeply disquieting than a conversation gone awry. To say something and see it taken to mean something else; to try to be helpful and be thought pushy; to try to be considerate and be called cold; to try to establish a rhythm so that talk will glide effortlessly about the room, only to end up feeling like a conversational clod who can't pick up the beat—such failure at talk undermines one's sense of competence and of being a right sort of person. If it happens continually, it can undermine one's feeling of psychological well-being.

This book gives a linguist's view of what makes conversation exhilarating or frustrating. Through the lens of linguistic analysis of conversational style, it shows how communication works—and fails to work. The aim is to let you know you're not alone and you're not crazy—and to give you more choice in continuing, ending, or improving communication in your private and public life.

To give you an idea of how a linguistic analysis of conversational style can help, I'll begin by describing how I learned to love linguistics and listen for style.

I got hooked on linguistics the year my marriage broke up.

Trying to turn a loss into a gain, I took advantage of my new-found freedom and attended the Linguistic Institute at the University of Michigan in the summer of 1973, to find out what linguistics was all about.

Seven years of living with the man I had just separated from had left me dizzy with questions about communication. What went wrong when we tried to talk to each other? Why did this wonderful, lovable man turn into a cruel lunatic when we tried to talk things out—and make me turn into one too?

I remember one argument near the end of our marriage. It stuck in my mind not because it was unique but because it was so painfully typical, and because the pitch of my frustration reached a new height. I felt I must be losing my mind. It was one of our frequent conversations about plans—simple plans, plans of no great consequence, but plans that involved us both and therefore had to be made in tandem. In this case it was about whether or not to accept an invitation to visit my sister.

I asked, cozy in the setting of our home and confident of my kindness in being willing to do whatever my husband wished, "Do you want to go to my sister's?" He answered, "Okay." I guess "Okay" didn't sound to me like an answer to my question; it seemed to indicate he was going along with something. So I followed up: "Do you really want to go?" He exploded. "You're driving me crazy! Why don't you make up your mind what you want?"

His explosion sent me into a tailspin. For one thing, I had learned from my father that even the nastiest impulses should be expressed quietly, so my husband's volume and intensity always scared me—and seemed morally wrong. But the reason I felt not so much angry as incredulous and out-raged was the seeming irrationality. (As Bruno Bettelheim has pointed out, people can put up with almost anything if they can see a reason for it.) "*My* mind? I haven't even said what I want. I'm willing to do whatever *you* want, and this is what I get?" I felt trapped in a theater of the absurd when I wanted desperately to live in a well-made play.

Reading this may give (to some) the impression that my husband was crazy. I thought he was. And I thought I was crazy for having married him. He was always getting angry at me for saying things I'd never said, or for not paying attention to things I was sure he had never said.

In the quiet of solitary thought and the recollected conviction of his good qualities, I'd decide that since we were both decent people who were generally well liked and otherwise showed no signs of mental disturbance, and since we loved each other, there was no reason for us to fight bitterly about nothing. I'd make up my mind that it wouldn't happen again. But then we'd start talking to each other, and sooner or later some insignificant comment would spark a heated response—and we'd be locking horns in irrational battle.

Linguistics to the Rescue

I had given up trying to solve these communication impasses but was still trying to understand how they'd developed, when I went to the Linguistic Institute. There I heard Professor Robin Lakoff lecture about indirectness. People prefer not to say exactly what they mean in so many words because they're not concerned only with the ideas they're expressing; they're also—even more—concerned with the effect their words will have on those they're talking to. They want to make sure to maintain camaraderie, to avoid imposing, and to give (or at least appear to give) the other person some choice in the matter being discussed. And different people have different ways of honoring these potentially conflicting goals.

A floodlight fell upon the stage of my marriage. I took it for granted that I would come out and say what I wanted, and that I could ask my husband what he wanted, and that he would tell me. When I asked if he wanted to visit my sister, I meant the question literally. I was asking for information about his preferences so I could accommodate them. Now he wanted to be accommodating too. But he assumed that people—even married people—don't go around just blurting out what they want. To him, that would be coercive because he found it hard to deny a direct request. So he assumed people hint at what they want and pick up hints.

A good way to hint is to ask a question. My husband saw, as clear as could be, that when I asked if he wanted to go to my sister's, I was letting him know that I wanted to go. Otherwise I wouldn't have brought it up. Since he agreed to give me what I wanted, I should have gracefully—and gratefully—accepted. When I followed up with a second question, "Are you sure you want to go?" he heard—again loud and clear—that I didn't want to go and was asking him to let me off the hook.

From my husband's point of view, I was being irrational. First I let him know that I wanted to go, and then when I got what I wanted, I changed my mind and let him know that I didn't want to go. He was trying to be agreeable, but I was being capricious—exactly my impression, but with our roles reversed. The intensity of his explosion (and of my reaction) came from the cumulative effect of repeated such frustrations.

Things like this happened to us so often that one of our private jokes was the protest: "I only did it for you." We could see the humor of this in retrospect, but when it happened, it was anything but funny.

We kept having conversations like this:

"We didn't go to the party because you didn't want to."
"I wanted to go. *You* didn't want to."

It would turn out that he had taken something I'd said as a hint about what I wanted, and I mistook his agreement with what he thought I wanted for being what he really wanted. He kept acting on hints I hadn't thrown out, and I kept missing hints he had. With both of us loaded with good will, we kept doing what neither wanted. And instead of thanks, we both got recriminations. We were driving each other crazy.

"Why?"

One of the biggest troublemakers in our marriage was the seemingly innocent little question "Why?" Having grown up in a family in which explanations were offered as a matter of course, I was always asking my husband, "Why?" He had grown up in a family in which explanations were neither offered nor sought, so when I asked, "Why?," he looked for hidden meaning—and concluded that I was questioning his decision and even his right to make it. My continually asking why seemed to him an effort to show him up as incompetent. Furthermore, not being accustomed to hearing people explain reasons for doing things, and not having been called upon to explain his reasons in the past, he tended to act on instinct. So he really couldn't have explained his reasons even if he'd wanted to.

As a result, we often had conversations like this:

> "Let's drop by Toliver's house tonight."
> "Why?"
> "All right, we don't have to go."

Then he would be angry at me for not being willing to do this small thing for him, and I'd be angry at him because he changed his mind on the spot, refused to explain either why he wanted to go or why he didn't, and inexplicably fell into a sulk.

What makes misunderstandings like these so hard to straighten out is that our ways of communicating seem self-evidently natural to us. He didn't feel he was hinting; he felt he was communicating. He didn't feel he was picking up hints from me; he felt he was hearing me communicate.

That's why the frequently heard advice to "be honest" doesn't help much. We *were* being honest. But our ways of being honest were different—and mutually unintelligible. When I missed his hint, he assumed I knew what he meant and refused to honor it. When I denied having meant what he heard me say (or heard me hint—the same thing), he thought I was being flighty or dishonest. Since I hadn't meant what he heard me say, and I hadn't heard what he knew he'd meant, our attempts to solve the problem were doomed. The only way we knew of treating the disease was precisely what was causing it—talking.

Spreading the Word

Having arrived at the Linguistic Institute in Ann Arbor with the confusion and frustration of years of such mixups fresh in my mind (and the pain of the breakup fresh in my heart), I began my study of linguistics by analyzing my own recollected miscommunications. I went on to get a doctorate in linguistics, and then to teach, lecture, and continue to investigate how normal use of language leads to seemingly abnormal misunderstandings, in private and in public.

Hearing accounts of these and other examples, friends and strangers who talked with me or attended my lectures, or who read my articles, kept telling me that they'd had the same kinds of misunderstandings. Again and again I heard, "You could've been talking about me and my husband" or "me and my boyfriend" or "me and my boss" or "me and my in-laws."

For example, Stephanie's mother-in-law had the habit of coming to visit with her dog: a cute but nervous and not yet house-trained little creature who barked at Stephanie's dog and caused a general ruckus. Stephanie tried politely to let her mother-in-law know that she didn't want her to bring the dog. She said, "You shouldn't bring your dog because it's not fair to him. He gets upset and barks at our dog, and then you have to lock him up, so he's not comfortable." The mother-in-law thanked Stephanie for her concern but assured her that the dog was fine during the visits. So Stephanie had to be more direct and say that *she* didn't like having the dog there. The mother-in-law didn't take offense, but Stephanie was angry because she felt her mother-in-law had forced her to be rude. She complained to her husband, Robert, "Why do I always have to spell things out for her?"

It wasn't until Stephanie heard my explanation of indirectness that it occurred to her that the problem was different conversational styles rather than her mother-in-law's obstinate character. She saw for the first time that what she had thought of as being polite was actually indirect and possibly not clear communication. For his part, Robert often offended and upset Stephanie's mother by being too direct, by saying, for example, "I don't want to do that" instead of "Well, I'll see what I can do," refusing only after giving the impression of having tried.

What some would call honesty was rudeness to Stephanie. For example, when a new friend, Linda, called to bow out of a dinner invitation by explaining she was just too tired, Stephanie was offended. Just being tired didn't seem sufficient reason to back out, so giving it as a reason seemed to show callousness toward the invitation. An appropriate excuse would have been that Linda didn't feel well or that something unexpected had come up—whether or not it was true. Stephanie never repeated the invitation, and she invented the appropriate excuses when Linda invited her. And that was the end of the budding friendship.

Talking Makes Our Worlds

In this way, our personal worlds are shaped by conversations—not only with family, friends, and co-workers but also in public. Whether the world seems a pleasant or a hostile place is largely the result of the cumulative impression of seemingly insignificant daily encounters: dealings with salespeople, bank clerks, letter carriers, bureaucratic officials, cashiers, and telephone operators. When these relatively minor exchanges are smooth and pleasant, we feel (without thinking about it) that we are doing things right. But when they are strained, confusing, or seemingly rude, our mood can be ruined and our energy drained. We wonder what's wrong with them—or us.

Indirectness, ways of using questions or refusing politely, are aspects of conversational style. We also send out signals by how fast we talk, how loudly, by our intonation and choice of words, as well as by what we actually say and when. These linguistic gears are always turning, driving our conversations, but we don't see them because we think in terms of intentions (rude, polite, interested) and character (she's nice, he's not).

Despite good intentions and good character all around—our own (which we take for granted) and others' (which we easily doubt)—we find ourselves caught in miscommunication because the very methods—and the only methods—we have of communicating are not, as they seem, self-evident and "logical." Instead, they differ from person to person, especially in a society like ours where individuals come from such varied cultural backgrounds.

A lot of seemingly inexplicable behavior—signs of coming closer or pulling back—occurs because others react to our style of talking in ways that lead them to conclusions we never suspect. Many of our motives, so obvious to us, are never perceived by the people we talk to. Many instances of rudeness, stubbornness, inconsiderateness, or refusal to co-operate are really caused by differences in conversational style.

What's to Be Done?

What can we do to avoid such misunderstandings in fleeting or intimate conversations? In some cases, we can alter our styles with certain other people. And we may try to clarify our intentions by explaining them, though that can be tricky. We usually don't know there has been a misunderstanding. And even if we do, few people are willing to go back and pick apart what they've just said or heard. Just letting others know that we're paying attention to how they talk can make them nervous. When Henry Higgins, in the opening scene of George Bernard Shaw's play *Pygmalion*, is seen taking notes on Eliza's accent, onlookers assume he is a policeman about to plunk her in jail.

Trying to be direct with someone who isn't used to it just makes things worse—as Stephanie felt angry that her mother-in-law forced her to be rude by "spelling things out." People intent on finding hidden meanings will look more and more desperately for the unexpressed intentions underlying our intended "direct" communication.

Often the most effective repair is to change the frame—the definition or the tone of what's going on—not by talking about it directly but by speaking in a different way, exhibiting different assumptions, and hence triggering different responses in the person we're talking to.

But the most important thing is to be aware that misunderstandings can arise, and with them tempers, when no one is crazy and no one is mean and no one is intentionally dishonest. We can learn to stop and remind ourselves that others may not mean what we heard them say.

I don't know if my marriage would have continued had I discovered linguistics before the breakup instead of right after. But I would have understood better what was going on, whether or not I wanted it to keep going on. And I wouldn't have thought, as I did in bad moments, that my husband was a Mr. Hyde, or that he or I or both of us were going, intermittently but unmistakably, crazy.

Life is a matter of dealing with other people, in little matters and cataclysmic ones, and that means a series of conversations. This book is meant to assure you that when conversations seem to be causing more problems than they're solving, you aren't losing your mind. And you may not have to lose (if you don't want to) your friendship, your partner, or your money to the ever-gaping jaws of differences in conversational style.

And now let's see what conversational style is and how it works.

CHAPTER TWO

The Workings of Conversational Style

The Meaning Is the Metamessage

You're sitting at a bar—or in a coffee shop or at a party—and suddenly you feel lonely. You wonder, "What do all these people find to talk about that's so important?" Usually the answer is, Nothing. Nothing that's so important. But people don't wait until they have something important to say in order to talk.

Very little of what is said is important for the information expressed in the words. But that doesn't mean that the talk isn't important. It's crucially important, as a way of showing that we are involved with each other, and how we feel about being involved. Our talk is saying something about our relationship.

Information conveyed by the meanings of words is the message. What is communicated about relationships—attitudes toward each other, the occasion, and what we are saying—is the metamessage. And it's metamessages that we react to most strongly. If someone says, "I'm not angry," and his jaw is set hard and his words seem to be squeezed out in a hiss, you won't believe the message that he's not angry;

you'll believe the metamessage conveyed by the way he said it—that he is. Comments like "It's not what you said but the way that you said it" or "Why did you say it like that?" or "Obviously it's not nothing; something's wrong" are responses to metamessages of talk.

Many of us dismiss talk that does not convey important information as worthless—meaningless small talk if it's a social setting or "empty rhetoric" if it's public. Such admonitions as "Skip the small talk," "Get to the point," or "Why don't you say what you mean?" may seem to be reasonable. But they are reasonable only if information is all that counts. This attitude toward talk ignores the fact that people are emotionally involved with each other and that talking is the major way we establish, maintain, monitor, and adjust our relationships.

Whereas words convey information, how we speak those words—how loud, how fast, with what intonation and emphasis—communicates what we think we're doing when we speak: teasing, flirting, explaining, or chastising; whether we're feeling friendly, angry, or quizzical; whether we want to get closer or back off. In other words, how we say what we say communicates social meanings.

Although we continually respond to social meaning in conversation, we have a hard time talking about it because it does not reside in the dictionary definitions of words, and most of us have unwavering faith in the gospel according to the dictionary. It is always difficult to talk about—even to see or think about—forces and processes for which we have no names, even if we feel their impact. Linguistics provides terms that describe the processes of communication and therefore make it possible to see, talk, and think about them.

This chapter introduces some of the linguistic terms that give names to concepts that are crucial for understanding communication—and therefore relationships. In addition to the concept of metamessages—underlying it, in a sense—there are universal human needs that motivate communication: the needs to be connected to others and to be left alone. Trying to honor these conflicting needs puts us in a double bind. The linguistic concept of politeness accounts for the way we serve these needs and react to the double bind—through metamessages in our talk.

Involvement and Independence

The philosopher Schopenhauer gave an often-quoted example of porcupines trying to get through a cold winter. They huddle together for warmth, but their sharp quills prick each other, so they pull away. But then they get cold. They have to keep adjusting their closeness and distance to keep from freezing and from getting pricked by their fellow porcupines—the source of both comfort and pain.

We need to get close to each other to have a sense of community, to feel we're not alone in the world. But we need to keep our distance from each other to preserve our independence, so others don't impose on or engulf us. This duality reflects the human condition. We are individual and social creatures. We need other people to survive, but we want to survive as individuals.

Another way to look at this duality is that we are all the same—and all different. There is comfort in being understood and pain in the impossibility of being understood completely. But there is also comfort in being different—special and unique—and pain in being the same as everyone else, just another cog on the wheel.

Valuing Involvement and Independence

We all keep balancing the needs for involvement and independence, but individuals as well as cultures place different relative values on these needs and have different ways of expressing those values. America as a nation has glorified individuality, especially for men. This is in stark contrast to people in many parts of the world outside Western Europe, who more often glorify involvement in family and clan, for women and men.

The independent pioneers—and later our image of them—have served us well. The glorification of independence served the general progress of the nation as (traditionally male) individuals have been willing to leave their hometowns—the comfort of the familiar and familial—to find opportunity, get the best education, travel, work wherever they could find the best jobs or wherever their jobs sent them. The yearning for involvement enticed (traditionally female) individuals to join them.

The values of the group are reflected in personal values. Many Americans, especially (but not only) American men, place more emphasis on their need for independence and less on their need for social involvement. This often entails paying less attention to the metamessage level of talk—the level that comments on relationships—focusing instead on the information level. The attitude may go as far as the conviction that only the information level really counts—or is really there. It is then a logical conclusion that talk not rich in information should be dispensed with. Thus, many daughters and sons of all ages, calling their parents, find that their fathers want to exchange whatever information is needed and then hang up, but their mothers want to chat, to "keep in touch."

American men's information-focused approach to talk has shaped the American way of doing business. Most Americans think it's best to "get down to brass tacks" as soon as possible, and not "waste time" in small talk (social talk) or "beating around the bush." But this doesn't work very well in business dealings with Greek, Japanese, or Arab counterparts for whom "small talk" is necessary to establish the social relationship that must provide the foundation for conducting business.

Another expression of this difference—one that costs American tourists huge amounts of money—is our inability to understand the logic behind bargaining. If the African, Indian, Arab, South American, or Mediterranean seller wants to sell a product, and the tourist wants to buy it, why not set a fair price and let the sale proceed? Because the sale is only one part of the interaction. Just as important, if not more so, is the interaction that goes on during bargaining: an artful way for buyer and seller to reaffirm their recognition that they're dealing with—and that they are—humans, not machines.

Believing that only the information level of communication is important and real also lets men down when it comes to maintaining personal relationships. From day to day, there often isn't any significant news to talk about. Women are negatively stereotyped as frivolously talking at length without conveying significant information. Yet their ability to keep talking to each other makes it possible for them to maintain close friendships. *Washington Post* columnist Richard Cohen observed that he and the other men he knows don't really have friends in the sense that women have them. This may be at least partly because they don't talk to each other if they can't think of some substantive topic to talk about. As a result, many men find themselves without personal contacts when they retire.

The Double Bind

No matter what relative value we place on involvement and independence, and how we express these values, people, like porcupines, are always balancing the conflicting needs for both. But the porcupine metaphor is a little misleading because it suggests a sequence: alternately drawing close and pulling back. Our needs for involvement and independence—to be connected and to be separate—are not sequential but simultaneous. We must serve both needs at once in all we say.

And that is why we find ourselves in a double bind. Anything we say to show we're involved with others is in itself a threat to our (and their) individuality. And anything we say to show we're keeping our distance from others is in itself a threat to our (and their) need for involvement. It's not just a conflict—feeling torn between two alternatives—or ambivalence—feeling two ways about one thing. It's a double bind because whatever we do to serve one need necessarily violates the other. And we can't step out of the circle. If we try to withdraw by not communicating, we hit the force field of our need for involvement and are hurled back in.

Because of this double bind, communication will never be perfect; we cannot reach stasis. We have no choice but to keep trying to balance independence and involvement, freedom and safety, the familiar and the strange—continually making adjustments as we list to one side or the other. The way we make these adjustments in our talk can be understood as politeness phenomena.

Information and Politeness in Talk

A language philosopher, H. P. Grice, codified the rules by which conversation would be constructed if information were its only point:

> Say as much as necessary and no more.
> Tell the truth.
> Be relevant.
> Be clear.

These make perfect sense—until we start to listen to and think about real conversations. For one thing, all the seeming absolutes underlying these injunctions are really relative. How much is necessary? Which truth? What is relevant? What is clear?

But even if we could agree on these values, we wouldn't want simply to blurt out what we mean, because we're juggling the needs for involvement and independence. If what we mean shows involvement, we want to temper it to show we're not imposing. If what we mean shows distance, we want to temper it with involvement to show we're not rejecting. If we state what we want or believe, others may not agree or may not want the same thing, so our statement could introduce disharmony; therefore we prefer to get an idea of what others want or think, or how they feel about what we want or think, before we commit ourselves to— maybe even before we make up our minds about—what we mean.

This broad concept of the social goals we serve when we talk is called "politeness" by linguists and anthropologists— not the pinky-in-the-air idea of politeness, but a deeper sense of trying to take into account the effect of what we say on other people.

Linguist Robin Lakoff devised another set of rules that describe the motivations behind politeness—that is, how we adjust what we say to take into account its effects on others. Here they are as Lakoff presents them:

1. Don't impose; keep your distance.
2. Give options; let the other person have a say.
3. Be friendly; maintain camaraderie.

Following Rule 3, Be friendly, makes others comfortable by serving their need for involvement. Following Rule 1, Don't impose, makes others comfortable by serving their need for independence. Rule 2, Give options, falls between Rules 1 and 3. People differ with respect to which rules they tend to apply, and when, and how.

To see how these rules work, let's consider a fairly trivial but common conversation. If you offer me something to drink, I may say, "No, thanks," even though I am thirsty. In some societies this is expected; you insist, and I give in after about the third offer. This is polite in the sense of Rule 1, Don't impose. If you expect this form of politeness and I accept on the first offer, you will think I'm too forward—or dying of thirst. If you don't expect this form of politeness, and I use it, you will take my refusal at face value—and I might indeed die of thirst while waiting for you to ask again.

I may also say, in response to your offer, "I'll have whatever you're having." This is polite in the sense of Rule 2, Give options: I'm letting you decide what to give me. If I do this, but you expect me to refuse the first offer, you may still think I'm pushy. But if you expect Rule 3, Be friendly, you may think me wishy-washy. Don't I know what I want?

Exercising Rule 3-style politeness, Be friendly, I might respond to your offer of something to drink by saying, "Yes, thanks, some apple juice, please." In fact, if this is my style of politeness, I might not wait for you to offer at all, but ask right off, "Have you got anything to drink?," or even head straight for your kitchen, throw open the refrigerator door, and call out, "Got any juice?"

If you and I both feel this is appropriate, my doing it will reinforce our rapport because we both subscribe to the rule of breaking rules; not having to follow the more formal rule sends a metamessage: "We are such good friends, we don't have to stand on ceremony." But if you don't subscribe to this brand of politeness, or don't want to get that chummy with me, you will be offended by my way of being friendly. If we have only recently met, that could be the beginning of the end of our friendship.

Of course, these aren't actually rules, but senses we have of the "natural" way to speak. We don't think of ourselves as following rules, or even (except in formal situations) of being polite. We simply talk in ways that seem obviously appropriate at the time they pop out of our mouths—seemingly self-evident ways of being a good person.

Yet our use of these "rules" is not unconscious. If asked

about why we said one thing or another in this way or that, we are likely to explain that we spoke the way we did "to be nice" or "friendly" or "considerate." These are commonsense terms for what linguists refer to, collectively, as politeness—ways of taking into account the effect on others of what we say.

The rules, or senses, of politeness are not mutually exclusive. We don't choose one and ignore the others. Rather we balance them all to be appropriately friendly without imposing, to keep appropriate distance without appearing aloof.

Negotiating the offer of a drink is a fairly trivial matter, though the importance of such fleeting conversations should not be underestimated. The way we talk in countless such daily encounters is part of what constitutes our image of ourselves, and it is on the basis of such encounters that we form our impressions of each other. They have a powerful cumulative effect on our personal and interactive lives.

Furthermore, the process of balancing these conflicting senses of politeness—serving involvement and independence—is the basis for the most consequential of interactions as well as the most trivial. Let's consider the linguistic means we have of serving these needs—and their inherent indeterminacy, which means they can easily let us down.

The Two-edged Sword of Politeness

Sue was planning to visit Amy in a distant city, but shortly before she was supposed to arrive, Sue called and canceled. Although Amy felt disappointed, she tried to be understanding. Being polite by not imposing, and respecting Sue's need for independence, Amy said it was really okay if Sue didn't come. Sue was very depressed at that time, and she got more depressed. She took Amy's considerateness—a sign of caring, respecting Sue's independence—as indifference—not caring at all, a lack of involvement. Amy later felt partly responsible for Sue's depression because she hadn't insisted that Sue visit. This confusion was easy to fall into and hard to climb out of because ways of showing caring and indifference are inherently ambiguous.

You can be nice to someone either by showing your involvement or by not imposing. And you can be mean by refusing to show involvement—cutting her off—or by imposing—being "inconsiderate." You can show someone you're angry by shouting at her—imposing—or refusing to talk to her at all: the silent activity called snubbing.

You can be kind by saying something or by saying nothing. For example, if someone has suffered a misfortune—failed an exam, lost a job, or contracted a disease—you may show sympathy by expressing your concern in words or by deliberately not mentioning it to avoid causing pain by bringing it up. If everyone takes the latter approach, silence becomes a chamber in which the ill, the bereaved, and the unemployed are isolated.

If you choose to avoid mentioning a misfortune, you run the risk of seeming to have forgotten, or of not caring. You may try to circumvent that interpretation by casting a knowing glance, making an indirect reference, or softening the impact with euphemisms ("your situation"), hedges and hesitations ("your . . . um . . . well . . . er . . . you know"), or apologies ("I hope you don't mind my mentioning this"). But meaningful glances and verbal hedging can themselves offend by sending the metamessage "This is too terrible to mention" or "Your condition is shameful." A person thus shielded may feel like shouting, "Why don't you just say it!?"

An American couple visited the husband's brother in Germany, where he was living with a German girlfriend. One evening during dinner, the girlfriend asked the brother where he had taken his American guests that day. Upon hearing that he had taken them to the concentration camp at Dachau, she exclaimed in revulsion that that was an awful place to take them; why would he do such a stupid thing?

The brother cut off her exclamations by whispering to her while glancing at the American woman. His girlfriend immediately stopped complaining and nodded in understanding, also casting glances at the American, who was not appreciative of their discretion. Instead, she was offended by the assumption that being Jewish is cause for whispering and furtive glances.

Any attempt to soften the impact of what is said can have the opposite effect. For example, a writer recalled the impression that a colleague had written something extremely critical about the manuscript of her book. Preparing to revise the manuscript, she returned to his comments and was surprised to see that the criticism was very mild indeed. The guilty word was the one that preceded the comment, not the comment itself. By beginning the sentence with "Frankly," her colleague sent a metamessage: "Steel yourself. This is going to hurt a lot."

Such layers of meaning are always at work in conversation; anything you say or don't say sends metamessages that become part of the meaning of the conversation.

Mixed Metamessages at Home

Parental love puts relative emphasis on involvement, but as children grow up, most parents give more and more signs of love by respecting their independence. Usually this comes too late for the children's tastes. The teenager who resents being told to put on a sweater or eat breakfast interprets the parent's sign of involvement as an imposition. Although this isn't in the message, the teenager hears a metamessage to the effect "You're still a child who needs to be told how to take care of yourself."

Partners in intimate relationships often differ about how they balance involvement and independence. There are those who show love by making sure the other eats right, dresses warmly, or doesn't drive alone at night. There are others who feel this is imposing and treating them like children. And there are those who feel that their partners don't care about them because they aren't concerned with what they eat, wear, or do. What may be meant as a show of respect for their independence is taken as lack of involvement—which it also might be.

Maxwell wants to be left alone, and Samantha wants attention. So she gives him attention, and he leaves her alone. The adage "Do unto others as you would have others do unto you" may be the source of a lot of anguish and misunderstanding if the doer and the done unto have different styles.

Samantha and Maxwell might feel differently if the other acted differently. He may want to be left alone precisely because she gives him so much attention, and she may want attention precisely because he leaves her alone. With a doting spouse she might find herself craving to be left alone, and with an independent spouse, he might find himself craving attention. It's important to remember that others' ways of talking to you are partly a reaction to your style, just as your style with them is partly a reaction to their style—with you.

The ways we show our involvement and considerateness in talk seem self-evidently appropriate. And in interpreting what others say, we assume they mean what we would mean if we said the same thing in the same way. If we don't think about differences in conversational style, we see no reason to question this. Nor do we question whether what we perceive as considerate or inconsiderate, loving or not, was *intended* to be so.

In trying to come to an understanding with someone who has misinterpreted our intentions, we often end up in a deadlock, reduced to childlike insistence:

> "You said so."
> "I said no such thing!"
> "You did! I heard you!"
> "Don't tell me what I said."

In fact, both parties may be sincere—and both may be right. He recalls what he meant, and she recalls what she heard. But what he intended was not what she understood—which was what she would have meant if she had said what he said in the way he said it.

These paradoxical metamessages are recursive and potentially confusing in all conversations. In a series of conversations between the same people, each encounter bears the burdens as well as the fruits of earlier ones. The fruits of ongoing relationships are an ever-increasing sense of understanding based on less and less talk. This is one of the great joys of intimate conversations. But the burdens include the incremental confusion and disappointment of past misunderstandings, and hardening conviction of the other's irrationality or ill will.

The benefits of repeated communication need no explanation; all our conventional wisdom about "getting to know each other," "working it out," and "speaking the same language" gives us ways to talk about and understand that happy situation. But we need some help—and some terms and concepts—to understand why communicating over time doesn't always result in understanding each other better, and why sometimes it begins to seem that one or the other is speaking in tongues.

Mixed Metamessages Across Cultures

The danger of misinterpretation is greatest, of course, among speakers who actually speak different native tongues, or come from different cultural backgrounds, because cultural difference necessarily implies different assumptions about natural and obvious ways to be polite.

Anthropologist Thomas Kochman gives the example of a white office worker who appeared with a bandaged arm and felt rejected because her black fellow worker didn't mention it. The (doubly) wounded worker assumed that her silent colleague didn't notice or didn't care. But the co-worker was purposely not calling attention to something her colleague might not want to talk about. She let her decide whether or not to mention it: being considerate by not imposing. Kochman says, based on his research, that these differences reflect recognizable black and white styles.

An American woman visiting England was repeatedly offended—even, on bad days, enraged—when Britishers ignored her in settings in which she thought they should pay attention. For example, she was sitting at a booth in a railroad-station cafeteria. A couple began to settle into the opposite seat in the same booth. They unloaded their luggage; they laid their coats on the seat; he asked what she would like to eat and went off to get it; she slid into the booth facing the American. And throughout all this, they showed no sign of having noticed that someone was already sitting in the booth.

When the British woman lit up a cigarette, the American had a concrete object for her anger. She began ostentatiously looking around for another table to move to. Of course there was none; that's why the British couple had sat in her booth in the first place. The smoker immediately crushed out her cigarette and apologized. This showed that she had noticed that someone else was sitting in the booth, and that she was not inclined to disturb her. But then she went back to pretending the American wasn't there, a ruse in which her husband collaborated when he returned with their food and they ate it.

To the American, politeness requires talk between strangers forced to share a booth in a cafeteria, if only a fleeting "Do you mind if I sit down?" or a conventional "Is anyone sitting here?" even if it's obvious no one is. The omission of such talk seemed to her like dreadful rudeness. The American couldn't see that another system of politeness was at work. (She could see nothing but red.) By not acknowledging her presence, the British couple freed her from the obligation to acknowledge theirs. The American expected a show of involvement; they were being polite by not imposing.

An American man who had lived for years in Japan explained a similar politeness ethic. He lived, as many Japanese do, in frightfully close quarters—a tiny room separated from neighboring rooms by paper-thin walls. In this case the walls were literally made of paper. In order to preserve privacy in this most unprivate situation, his Japanese neighbors simply acted as if no one else lived there. They never showed signs of having overheard conversations, and if, while walking down the hall, they caught a neighbor with the door open, they steadfastly glued their gaze ahead as if they were alone in a desert. The American confessed to feeling what I believe most Americans would feel if a next-door neighbor passed within a few feet without acknowledging their presence—snubbed. But he realized that the intention was not rudeness by omitting to show involvement, but politeness by not imposing.

The fate of the earth depends on cross-cultural communication. Nations must reach agreements, and agreements are made by individual representatives of nations sitting down and talking to each other—public analogues of private conversations. The processes are the same, and so are the pitfalls. Only the possible consequences are more extreme.

We Need the Eggs

Despite the fact that talking to each other frequently fails to yield the understanding we seek, we keep at it, just as nations keep trying to negotiate and reach agreement. Woody Allen knows why, and tells, in his film *Annie Hall*, which ends with a joke that is heard voice over:

> This guy goes to a psychiatrist and says, "Doc, my brother's crazy. He thinks he's a chicken." And the doctor says, "Well, why don't you turn him in?" And the guy says, "I would, but I need the eggs." Well, I guess that's pretty much how I feel about relationships.

Even though intimate as well as fleeting conversations don't yield the perfect communication we crave—and we can see from past experience and from the analysis presented here that they can't—we still keep hoping and trying because we need the eggs of involvement and independence. The communication chicken can't give us these golden eggs because of the double bind: Closeness threatens our lives as individuals, and our real differences as individuals threaten our needs to be connected to other people.

But because we can't step out of the situation—the human situation—we keep trying to balance these needs. We do it by not saying exactly what we mean in our messages, while at the same time negotiating what we mean in metamessages. Metamessages depend for their meaning on subtle linguistic signals and devices. These signals and devices, and how they work (or fail to), are presented and explained in the next chapter.

CHAPTER THREE

Conversational Signals and Devices

When we open our mouths to say something, we usually feel we are just talking, but what we say and how we say it are chosen from a great range of possibilities. And others react to our choices, just as they react to the clothes we wear, which serve the practical purpose of covering us up and keeping us warm, but also give impressions about the kind of people we are, and our attitudes toward the occasion. Wearing a three-piece suit may signal a formal (or stuffy) style or respect for the occasion; wearing jeans may signal a casual (or scruffy) style or not taking the occasion seriously. Personalities like formal and casual, stuffy and scruffy, and attitudes like respect or lack of it are also signaled by ways of talking.

Everything that is said must be said in some way—in some tone of voice, at some rate of speed, with some intonation and loudness. We may or may not consciously consider *what* to say before speaking. Rarely do we consciously consider *how* to say it, unless the situation is obviously loaded: for example, a job interview, a public address, firing someone, or breaking off a personal relationship. And we almost never make deliberate decisions about whether to raise or lower our voice and pitch, whether to speed up or slow down. But these are the signals by which we interpret each other's meaning and decide what we think of each other's comments—and each other.

Conversational style isn't something extra, added on like frosting on a cake. It's the very stuff of which the communication cake is made. Aspects of conversational style are the basic tools of talk—the way we show what we mean when we say (or don't say) something. The main signals are pacing and pausing, loudness, and pitch, all of which make up what is commonly thought of as intonation.

These signals are used in linguistic devices that do the work of conversation, complex work that includes, always and simultaneously: creating conversation by taking turns talking; showing how ideas are related to each other; showing what we think we are doing when we talk (for example, we're listening, interested, appreciative, friendly, seeking help, or offering it); and revealing how we feel at the time we're talking.

First, I describe what conversational signals are, how they work, and how they can wreak havoc when speakers have different habits about how and when to use them. The signals discussed are pacing and pausing; loudness; and pitch and intonation. Second, I present some examples of how these signals combine to make up conversational devices: expressive reaction, asking questions, complaining, and apologizing—and how they can be used successfully (when styles are shared) or unsuccessfully (when styles differ).

PART I: CONVERSATIONAL SIGNALS

"Hold Your Horses!"/"What Are You Waiting For?": *Pacing and Pausing*

Sara tried to befriend her old friend Steve's new wife, but Betty never seemed to have anything to say. While Sara felt Betty didn't hold up her end of the conversation, Betty complained to Steve that Sara never gave her a chance to talk. The problem had to do with expectations about pacing and pausing.

Conversation is a turn-taking game. You talk, then I talk, then you talk again. One person starts talking when another is finished. That seems simple enough.

But how do you know when I'm finished? Well, when I stop. But how do you know when I'm stopping? When my voice gets softer, when I start repeating myself, or when I slow down and leave a gap at the end.

But how soft does my voice have to get to mean "That's about it" as opposed to "This isn't the main point yet" or "I'm a mumbler"? Does repeating myself mean "I'm out of new things to say" or "I'm emphasizing"? And how much of a gap after a word means "I'm stopping" as opposed to "I'm pausing within my turn"—pausing for breath, to find the right words, for dramatic effect, or, as with any conversational signal, just out of habit?

In the midst of a conversation, you don't take time to puzzle this out. You sense when I'm finished, or about to make a point, or chatting aimlessly, based on your years of experience talking to people. When our habits are similar, there's no problem. What you sense and what I feel are similar. But if our habits are different, you may start to talk before I'm finished—in other words, interrupt—or fail to take your turn when I *am* finished—leading me to observe that you're not paying attention or have nothing to say.

That's what was happening with Betty and Sara. The tiny pause for which Betty kept waiting never occurred when Sara was around, because before it did, Sara sensed an awkward silence and kindly ended it by filling the gap with more talk—hers. And when Betty did start to say something, she tended to have what seemed to Sara like long pauses within her speech, giving Sara the impression that Betty was finished when she had hardly gotten started.

Such differences are not a matter of some people expecting long pauses and others expecting short ones. Long and short are relative; they have meaning only in comparison to something—what's expected, or someone else's pause. Someone who expects a shorter pause than the person she's speaking to will often start talking before the other has a chance to finish or to start. Someone who is waiting for a longer pause than the person she's speaking to won't be able to get a word in edgewise.

When Bob, who is from Detroit, talks to his colleagues from New York City, he keeps getting interrupted because he waits longer than they between turns. But in conversations with Athabaskan Indians in Alaska, where he works, he finds that he is doing all the talking—because Athabaskans expect longer pauses between turns than he does. With New Yorkers, Bob is a slow talker; with Athabaskans, he's a fast talker.

A woman from Texas went to Washington D.C. for a job in dormitory administration. When the dorm staff got together for meetings, she kept searching for the right time to break in—and never found it. Although back home she was considered outgoing and confident, in Washington she was perceived as shy and retiring. When she was evaluated at the end of a year, she was told to take an assertiveness-training course because of her inability to speak up.

That's why slight differences in conversational style—tiny little things like microseconds of pause—can have enormous impact on your life. These little signals make up the mechanics of conversation, and when they're even slightly off, conversation is thrown off—or even cut off. The result in this case was a judgment of psychological problems—even in the mind of the woman herself, who really wondered what was wrong with her and signed up for assertiveness training.

"Who's Shouting?"/"Why Are You Whispering?": *Loudness*

Another problem between Sara and Betty was that in Sara's view, Betty always whispered. And Betty was aghast when Steve got together with Sara and many of his other friends and family, because they always seemed angry—shouting at each other in the most appalling way. The problem here was different expectations about how loud it's normal to talk.

Anything you say has to be said at some level of loudness or softness, and as you speak, that level can go up or down. Getting louder can show the relationship between ideas ("This point is important"), or serve as a switching signal ("Wait, I want to say something"; "Wait, I'm not finished yet") or express emotions ("I'm angry"; "I'm excited"). Getting softer can reflect the parallel meanings: "This point is by-the-way" (a spoken equivalent of parentheses) or "I've run out of steam; you can take over" or "I feel too bad or embarrassed about this to say it any louder." Speaking softly can also be a sign of respect—for example, at a funeral or when speaking to those of more advanced age or status.

Because loudness can signal all these different intentions, confusion may arise about its meaning. For example, Alice lowers her voice when telling Carolyn something about her husband. Carolyn asks why Alice feels so bad about it—and Alice says she doesn't feel bad; she's keeping her voice down because he's in the next room. But things can get really confused in conversations among individuals who have different ideas about how and when to use loudness and softness—and about how loud is loud.

A native New Yorker never realized she was slightly hard of hearing until she moved to the Midwest. She frequently couldn't hear what people were saying when they sat across the table from her. In New York she rarely had trouble hearing anyone in the same room.

When you hear others talking more loudly than you expect, they seem to be shouting—and seem angry or brash. When you hear others talking more softly than you expect, they seem to be whispering—and withholding or unassertive. If they use loudness at unexpected points in their talk, you can get confused about what's important, or even what the point is. If you expect extra loudness to express emotion—for example, anger—and you don't hear it, you may not notice when those with different styles are angry. If you discover they are, you may think there's something wrong with them for not expressing it in what seems to you a normal way.

For example, Joe was shocked to learn that his office manager, Murray, was angry at him. Murray never raised his voice nor showed emotion in it. It turned out that Murray had been expressing his anger by not talking to Joe. Joe didn't get the message; he thought that Murray was just very busy. (For his part, Murray never neglects to stop and chat, no matter how busy he is, and Joe's habit of rushing by when he's busy hurts Murray's feelings and makes him suspect that Joe is angry at him when he's not.)

When Joe learned that Murray was angry at him, he concluded that Murray couldn't be trusted to let people know what was on his mind. That's the tragedy of crossed conversational signals. Joe thinks there's something wrong with Murray—any normal person would show emotion in his voice when angry. And Murray thinks there's something wrong with Joe: "How dare he shout at me?" Neither can see the logic in the other's system nor the relativity of his own.

Business As Usual/Expression of Emotion: Pitch and Intonation

A Greek man married to an American woman accused her of speaking in an irritating monotone, especially when their tempers were strained. She felt terrible about this newly discovered failing, and wondered why no one had ever mentioned it before. It never occurred to either of them that he found the tune of her talk monotonous because he was listening for the extreme shifts in pitch typical of Greek speakers, especially Greek women. And her American habit of muting her expression of emotion when she was upset seemed unnatural to him.

The music of talk, or intonation, comes from the combination of pacing, pausing, loudness, and maybe most of all, changes in pitch. Our voices have different absolute pitches; physical makeup determines that. And women tend to have higher-pitched voices than men. But as with loudness and pacing, what's significant is not absolute but comparative values—what we do with the pitches we've got.

Changing the pitch on a word can change the metamessage of the words spoken. Like loudness and softness, it can signal relative meaning, turn switching, or emotions.

Pitch shifts are a basic tool for signaling meaning. For example, pitch going up at the end of a sentence can make the sentence into a question. But it can also show uncertainty or ask for approval. And these meanings can be confused. Robin Lakoff observed that many women use rising intonation to be agreeable. When asked "What would you like to drink?," a woman answering "White wine?" may mean "White wine, if that's convenient" but be taken to mean "I think I want white wine but I'm not sure."

Some people, in telling about their experiences, use rising intonation at the end of each phrase. This encourages their listeners to say "uh-huh" or "mhm" more frequently, but it may also give the impression they're fishing for approval or verification.

Some people (and most people from some cultures) send their voices way up and way down in pitch. These shifts show their attitudes toward what they're saying and also show that they care, that they're emotionally involved.

Lois asked Peter, in a dinner-table conversation I taped, what book he was reading. He gave the title, which was an odd one. With high pitch, Lois asked, *"What's that?"* Her high pitch seemed to imply (with a good-natured irony typical of her style): "That's a weird thing to read." Peter showed he understood and appreciated her irony by matching her extreme use of pitch shifts. He responded:

His pitch was fairly high on "It's" and went very low on "a novel," implying that he didn't take what he was reading very seriously. Then, to show he really does have good taste, he told of reading novels by John Fowles about whom he said, "He's a great writer. I think he's one of the best writers." His pitch was very high at the beginning of each sentence and went very low at the ends:

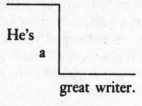

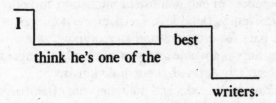

think he's one of the best writers.

The effect was to convey great sincerity and earnestness.

If you expect extreme shifts in pitch and don't hear them, what you hear sounds monotonous. You get the impression that the speaker is a bland sort of person, or doesn't care much about this conversation, or even is emotionally disturbed, suffering from "flattened affect." If you don't expect such extreme pitch shifts and you hear them, you may conclude that the person is overdramatizing or overemotional.

Since signals such as pitch shifts (as well as loudness and pacing) are also signs of emotional expression, it is probably no coincidence that women tend to use greater shifts in pitch than men, and that women are often perceived as overemotional. The same goes for members of certain cultural groups, including Greeks. Bearing this in mind, psychiatrists, psychologists, and social workers, whose jobs entail assessing the appropriateness of levels of emotional expression, must make efforts not to take their own conversational styles as universal norms. Expressing too little emotion is a symptom of repression or, in its most extreme form, catatonia. Expressing too much emotion is evidence of hostility or hysteria. A Japanese woman who not only doesn't cry but laughs when talking about her husband's death might be misdiagnosed by a Westerner who does not know that laughter is the customary and expected Japanese way of masking emotions. Medical doctors, too, have a difficult task determining the extent of pain felt by patients of different cultures. Patients of Mediterranean background may show extreme reactions while experiencing far less pain than is being felt by an American Indian who is rigid and silent.

Cultural differences in habitual use of intonation and other means of expressiveness (loudness, facial expression, gesturing) account in part for cross-cultural stereotyping, which is simply the extension to a whole group of the kinds of impressions that are regularly formed about individuals.

Our impressions of rudeness and politeness are often based on subtle variations in pitch. All conversation, in addition to whatever else it does, displays, and asks for recognition of, our competence. Little shifts in pitch can make us feel that others are questioning our abilities. For example, if you call the telephone operator and tell her you had trouble reaching a number, she will probably say something like "What's the number, please." But if her pitch goes up on "number," she sounds impatient; she seems to be implying you should have told her the number already. The impression that the operator is (without justification) annoyed at you will probably make you annoyed at her.

Finally, different uses of pitch to signal turn switches were partly responsible for Sara's cutting Betty off before she had said what she had in mind. Betty's pitch tended to drop at the end of each phrase, a signal that, to Sara, means "I'm finished; you take over." Not knowing Sara was reacting to her own signal, Betty felt interrupted.

Thus conversational signals can get crossed when well-intentioned speakers have different habits and expectations about using pacing and pausing, loudness, and pitch to show their intentions through talk—in other words, different conversational styles.

PART II:
CONVERSATIONAL DEVICES AT WORK

Conversational signals are used in devices that do the daily work of having conversations—work like showing you're listening, interested, establishing solidarity—or that you're not. Usually these devices work just fine, but because they're not explicit, they can be misinterpreted. Let's consider four conversational devices: expressive reaction, asking questions, complaining, and apologizing.

1. "I'm Listening"/"You're Nuts": Expressive Reaction

In a dinner-table conversation I taped and studied among Chad and David and Jonathan and Nora, Chad and David kept stumbling and stalling. One of the reasons, I discovered in the study, was the loud responses they were getting from Jonathan and Nora—responses that, ironically, were intended to encourage them.

For example, Chad made a point and Nora yelled, loud and fast, "WOW!" and Jonathan exclaimed, "OH, MY GOD!" They were using loudness and fast pace to show that they were really listening, that they got the point, and that it was a point well worth getting. But instead of encouraging Chad, these expressive responses pulled him up short. The loudness and quickness scared him and made him stop to find out what had caused the outburst.

David tended to be put off by such loud responses too. In fact, he often felt hurt by Jonathan's way of reacting to things he told him. For example, if David complained to Jonathan about something someone else had said, Jonathan might exclaim, his voice thick with scorn, "That's ridiculous!" This sounded to David as if Jonathan were questioning his veracity: If it was so ridiculous, it must not have happened the way David said it did. It made David wonder whether he really was remembering right, even though he knew he was—the "Am I crazy or what?" reaction that's common when conversational styles differ. And David blamed Jonathan for causing him self-doubt and discomfort.

But Jonathan wasn't questioning David's story. Quite the

opposite. His response was intended to show solidarity with David and appreciation for his story. The disbelief was aimed not at David but at the person about whom David was complaining, so the metamessage to David was intended to be "I agree that this other guy is ridiculous; this story is really worth telling, and I'm on your side."

Differences in expectations about how much of a reaction is appropriate can exist even within a family. A woman who had grown up in New York had raised her own children in Vermont. Often when her daughter told her about things that happened at school, the mother reacted with what seemed to her appropriate appreciation—but the daughter was startled and looked around to see what had provoked such a strong reaction in her mother. When she realized her mother was simply responding to her story, the daughter groaned, "Oh, Mom!"—certain (as adolescents so often are) that her mother was exhibiting an idiosyncratic overreaction.

The daughter in this example, like David in the preceding one, was getting more of a reaction than expected. The flip side of such differences is getting less reaction than expected and hence the impression that the toned-down listener isn't listening, isn't following, or isn't interested. When this happens on the telephone, you may actually ask, "Are you still there?"

2. When Is Interest Interrogation?
Asking Questions

Another way of showing interest and appreciation is asking questions. But questions can also seem nosy, overbearing, or hinting at something else. Questions, like everything we say, work on two levels at once: the message and the meta-message.

The message of a question is a request for information. In some contexts, that's the most important part—for example, when you stop a stranger in the street to ask directions, or when a policeman or lawyer questions a witness. (Though actually policemen and lawyers make judgments about witnesses and suspects based on the way they answer, listening for metamessages.)

We are most consciously aware of the message work of questions—their job of getting information. But in casual conversation, questions do just as much if not more of other types of work—for example, covering for less acceptable speech actions like criticizing or giving orders. Instead of saying "Don't do that!" people ask "What are you doing?" or "Why are you doing that?" Or, as in the example in Chapter One, instead of saying "I don't want to go with you," one could ask "Why do you want to go?"

Just as any conversational device can serve independence or involvement and can be seen to violate either, so questions can be used and understood to show interest or imposition.

Richard doesn't like to visit Lucy's family because he feels they ask him too many questions: He feels interrogated. One thing Richard could do to stop the interrogation is something he never thinks of doing: asking them lots of questions. He'll never do that because it would feel rude to him.

Lucy doesn't like to visit Richard's family because they never ask her any questions, so she feels they aren't interested in her. One time Lucy decided, almost out of spite, to talk about what was going on at work anyway—just to entertain herself. She was amazed to see that they listened attentively and seemed glad to hear about it.

Lucy's family tend to ask questions to show interest, but many people are more like Richard's family. For example, Lucy's sister Carol had dinner with a young man she had recently met. He seemed rather reticent, but Carol did her best to keep the conversation going and show interest in him. At the end of the evening the young man said, "It was nice having dinner with the FBI."

Not only did Carol ask questions to show interest, but she

asked them in a way that sounded to her new (and soon to be erstwhile) friend like machine-gun fire. She used signals such as loudness, fast pacing, and clipped wording to toss questions out quickly (for example, "Whaddya do? Y'an artist?"). She meant thus to send a metamessage of casual friendliness. But instead of making him feel relaxed, her rapid-fire questions made him feel under interrogation. His extreme reticence, which was a reaction to her questions, was making her ask more, since asking questions was her instinctive way of getting a conversation going.

Some people show interest by asking questions, and others expect people to volunteer what they want to say. Some people encourage others to talk by getting the ball rolling themselves. Others wait to be asked. If Mary is waiting to be asked, and John is waiting for her to volunteer, she will never talk—and each will blame the other for the resulting imbalance.

3. The Art of Ritual Complaining

Another conversational device is complaining, and it too can be used in different ways.

Jane and Sharon were talking about their mothers' holiday visits. Jane told Sharon that hers had been a bit trying because her mother complained a lot and made comments that were critical of Jane. Sharon told Jane that hers had been terrific; her mother was always optimistic, and even if she said things that could be seen as offensive, Sharon didn't take offense because she knew her mother meant well. Jane began to feel uncomfortable. She regretted talking against her mother and wanted to take it all back. Her mother also meant well and furthermore she was warm and youthful and generous!

Jane's discomfort arose because Sharon didn't respond to her complaint the way she expected—with a matching complaint, sending the metamessage "You're not alone; your mother is just a typical mother; I'm in the same boat." Instead, the metamessage Jane heard was "You've really got a rotten mother, you poor thing. Mine is much better." That made Jane want to retort, "She is *not*. Mine's better!"

Jane was (without thinking it through) trying to play a game of sharing complaints. But Sharon's response felt to her like a game of one-upmanship. To Sharon, complaining about one's mother is not only not expected; it's bad form. Ironically, and not coincidentally, both Sharon and Jane were talking in the ways they ascribed to their mothers—Sharon was stressing the positive, and Jane was trying to establish solidarity by complaining.

Rick and Lenny are journalists at the same newspaper. One day Lenny ribbed Rick by telling a third colleague that Rick always comes into his office and complains about being overworked, but then refuses to turn down assignments or avoid talking to the innumerable pests who call asking for free information. Instead of smiling, Rick was hurt and said seriously, "I'll never complain to you again." Then Lenny was hurt and said seriously, "I hope you don't mean that."

Lenny and Rick had different notions of ritual complaining. Lenny was advertising the fact that Rick complains to him as a sign of their friendship, and complaining about Rick in front of someone else (a form of teasing) was a sign of solidarity with both of them. But to Rick, Lenny's complaining to a third party was a violation of trust. They had different senses of when and how to use the device, complaining.

4. "First Me, Then You": Setting a Good Example

Self-revelation, asking questions, and complaining can all be used according to the conversational principle "Do as I do."

The expectation that others will follow suit explains what otherwise seems like irrational or even hypocritical conversational behavior.

A woman was having lunch with a man she had recently met who regaled her with stories about himself. In exasperation, she finally protested, "Why are you telling me all this?" He explained, "I want to get to know you." To her this was patently absurd. How could he get to know her by talking about himself? Simple—if he assumed that his personal revelations would encourage her to follow suit. When they didn't, he tried harder and harder, telling more and more personal stories to show how acceptable it was. If she refused to do her part, it wasn't for lack of trying on his.

Myrna and Lillian were trying to clear up a misunderstanding. Lillian had invited Myrna to drop by for a visit and to bring a mutual friend; Myrna had accepted the invitation and brought him over. But it turned out that Lillian hadn't meant the invitation literally; she had expected Myrna, based on prior conversations as well as the way the invitation was offered, to realize it was *pro forma* and turn it down. After a somewhat strained conversation in which both women explained how they had acted and felt, Myrna apologized: "Well, I'm sorry I didn't get your hint. Maybe I tend to take what people say too literally." Lillian accepted Myrna's apology: "Yes, I've often noticed you do that." Instead of ending the disagreement, this made Myrna angry all over again.

Myrna didn't really believe she had been at fault. Then why did she apologize? It was a gesture of good will, a conventionalized way to show she was ready to end the discussion—and the disagreement—like a ritual handshake. She expected Lillian to do the same, saying something like "I'm sorry too. I guess I tend to be too indirect" or "take too much for granted" or any formulation of her behavior that claimed part of the responsibility. Myrna expected disagreements to end with both parties claiming partial—but only partial—culpability. Lillian's accepting her apology rather than matching it seemed to interpret it as literal rather than ritual, thereby reinvoking the question of who was really at fault.

The Gears of Conversation

These are some typical ways the conversational signals of pacing, pausing, loudness, and pitch are used to carry on the business of taking turns in conversation; relating ideas to each other and showing what the point is; and showing how we feel about what we're saying and about the person we're saying it to. These are the signals that combine with what is said to make up the devices we use to show we're listening, interested, sympathetic, or teasing—and that we're the right sort of people.

These conversational signals and devices are normally invisible, the silent and hidden gears that drive conversations. We don't pay attention to the gears unless something seems to have gone wrong. Then we may ask "What do you *mean* by that?" And even then we don't think in terms of the signals—"Why did your pitch go up?"—but in terms of intentions—"Why are you angry?"

Many of these signals and devices can be changed if we're aware of them, either across the board or with certain others. And minor changes can have major results. For example, when conversations just don't seem to be going well, we can try making little adjustments in our volume, pacing, or pitch—speeding up or slowing down, leaving longer pauses or shorter ones—in an attempt to get closer to a shared rhythm. And realizing that ritual complaining and apologizing do not have the same meaning for everyone, we can be alert to others' reactions. When using these devices doesn't spark the reaction we expect, we can refrain from using them in the future with those others rather than drawing negative conclusions about their personalities—for example, that they are smug and self-satisfied—or that they have bad intentions toward us—for example, that they're one-upping us.

Adjustments of this type can correct after the fact, but not prevent, misunderstandings due to differences in conversational style. In a heterogeneous society, the signals and devices described in this chapter, seemingly minor phenomena, are likely to cause major disruptions and misunderstandings in ongoing or fleeting, intimate or public, one-time-only or day-to-day conversations. We can't stop using them, because they are the basic tools with which we build strategies for balancing involvement and independence when we talk to each other. When differing habits for using these tools lead to disagreements, people find themselves challenging others, in frustration: "Why don't you say what you mean?" The next chapter explains why, even when we want to be honest, we often don't say what we mean.

II.

Conversational Strategies

CHAPTER FOUR

Why We Don't Say What We Mean

T he conversational signals described in Chapter Three make up the *how* of talk. *What* we say is also an important clue to what we mean, but we don't always say what we mean in so many words. We balance the conflicting needs for involvement and independence by hinting and picking up hints, by refraining from saying some things and surmising what other people mean from what they refrain from saying. Linguists refer to the way people mean what they don't exactly say as *indirectness*.

Many people, especially Americans, tend to associate indirectness with dishonesty and directness with honesty, a quality we see as self-evidently desirable. In explaining why the press pursued the issue of Debategate—Reagan's campaign officials' obtaining copies of Carter debate documents—the executive producer of the *CBS Evening News* is quoted as saying, "Had the president handled the press conference more directly, we might not have gone back to the story."

"Not handling directly" here implies not telling the whole story—that is, not telling the truth.

In most day-to-day situations, this view of indirectness as dishonest is not fair, and not realistic. As we talk to each other about important or unimportant matters, we are always monitoring our relationships to each other, and information about relationships is found in metamessages, which by definition are not spelled out in words but signaled by the way words are spoken. So indirectness, in the sense of metamessages, is basic to communication. Everything must be said in some way; the way it is said sends metamessages—indirectly.

There are two big payoffs to being understood without saying explicitly what we mean: payoffs in rapport and in self-defense. And there's an aesthetic pleasure in communicating cryptically. These benefits of indirectness are the subject of the first part of this chapter. The second part explains why we can't be direct, even if we wanted to.

PART I:
WHY WE *WON'T* SAY WHAT WE MEAN
The Metamessage of Rapport

Cynthia told Greg she was hurt because he fixed himself a snack without offering her any. So he offered her the snack he had just fixed. She turned it down. He asked why. Because he hadn't prepared it for her. Greg was exasperated: Was she hungry or not?

To Cynthia, whether or not she was hungry was beside the point; the point was whether or not Greg thought about her when he fixed himself a snack, which showed whether or not he cared about her as much as she cared about him. She would never feed herself without asking him "Would you like some?" In fact, she might not even have a snack if he didn't want one.

Being direct and honest wouldn't help here. Cynthia could say straight out that she's hungry—or isn't—but that has nothing to do with it. She could say straight out that she wants to know Greg cares. But she can only know he cares if he thinks of her on his own. What good is it if you order someone to say "I love you," and he parrots it? It's no good at all telling people what you want if what you want is for them to know without your telling them. That's the rapport benefit of indirectness.

This drama is played out in the birthday-present routine. Anyone could get you what you want for your birthday if you told him what you want. In fact, you could get it for yourself, if it were the gift (the message) that mattered. What really matters is the metamessage: evidence that the person knows you well enough to figure out what you would like, and cares enough to spend the time getting it.

Nancy had mentioned her intention of buying a certain pair of work gloves, which were sold in the store in town. She felt cheated of a birthday present when, on her birthday, Thomas presented her with a pair of those gloves, which he had asked their neighbors to pick up when they drove into town. Nancy felt Thomas should have taken the trouble to figure out on his own something she would like, and pick it out—and up—himself.

Birthdays, like Christmas, can be setups for disappointment because so much seems to hang on the metamessages of gifts from those one is close to. But indirectness works very well in most situations, if people agree on how to use it.

A Greek woman explained how she and her father (and later her husband) communicated. If she wanted to do something, like go to a dance, she had to ask her father for permission. He never said no. But she could tell from the way he said yes whether or not he meant it. If he said something like "Yes, of course, go," then she knew he thought it was a good idea. If he said something like "If you want, you can go," then she understood that he didn't think it was a good idea, and she wouldn't go. His tone of voice, facial expression, and all the elements of conversational style gave her clues as to how he felt about her going.

Why didn't he just tell her that he didn't think she should go? Why wasn't he "honest"? Well, he *did* tell her, in a way that was clear to both her and him. To the extent that we can even talk about honesty in communicative habits, any system that successfully gets meaning across is honest.

It's easy to see that the Greek father might prefer not to appear tyrannical. What's more, he might not *feel* tyrannical, but might genuinely feel that he didn't say no; his daughter chose not to go of her own free will. How much better to have a daughter who chooses to behave properly rather than one who simply obeys. And the daughter herself might prefer it to appear that she is choosing not to go. In fact, she may actually feel that she is choosing, since her father never actually said she couldn't go. How much better to choose to act properly than to be forced into obeying. So the indirectness of their communication contributes to the appearance, and probably also the feeling, of rapport.

The Protective Armor of Indirectness

Another benefit to both father and daughter in this example is self-defense: avoiding confrontation. She hasn't gone on record as wanting to go to the party; she just asked. And he hasn't gone on record as refusing permission. If they disagree, it hasn't been stated, and both can save face, no matter what happens. If the daughter goes anyway, she needn't openly defy her father. If she doesn't go, she can console herself with a sour grapes "I didn't really want to go anyway."

The self-defense benefit of indirectness accounts for the logic by which we ask pre-questions like "Are you busy tonight?" It protects us from rejection by refusal once we have committed ourselves to an invitation.

The Danger of Indirectness

In the case of the Greek father and daughter, the system worked. But when one person is expressing intentions without going on record and the other expects to hear the information expressed outright, or expects different indirect signals and devices, the field is ripe for misunderstanding.

Imagine that a Greek-American cousin who speaks Greek comes to visit the family. She asks her uncle if she can go to a dance, and he says yes in the way his daughter always understands to mean he's not crazy about the idea. The cousin takes his equivocal response at face value and goes to the dance. It's like speaking different languages, only worse, because they think they're speaking the same language. The Greek uncle finds his American niece (and maybe all American young women) willful and disobedient—and even morally loose. The niece, faced with her uncle's subsequent disapproval, finds him (and maybe all Greek men) inconsistent and irascible.

Just Joking

There are many ways of saying one thing and meaning another. Irony, sarcasm, and figures of speech are such devices, and they are wonderful when they work. Joking is a kind of irony that has both rapport and defensive payoffs. The rapport benefit lies in the sensual pleasure of shared laughter as well as the evidence of rapport in having matching senses of humor. The defensive benefit is in the ability to retreat: "I was only joking."

We can see the complex metamessages of joking, and its indirect nature, in the following segment from the novel

Household Words by Joan Silber. In this scene, Moe reacts with ironic humor when Rhoda will neck with him but won't "go all the way":

> He would get up and hop about, kicking down the cuffs of his trousers, and moaning, "It only hurts when I walk, for instance. Who needs to walk?" He clutched himself in mockery of his own discomfort. It became a sort of family joke between them.

If you look at the words he speaks, you might conclude that Moe isn't saying what he means. Yet he is actually saying just what he means, which is far more than the information conveyed. That sexual play without intercourse makes him physically uncomfortable is clear, even though he doesn't say it. That his physical discomfort is not intolerable is shown by his joking about it—and by the obvious fact that, contrary to what he says, he is able to walk.

Moreover, there is a metamessage of good will in Moe's good humor. That he goes through the same joking routine regularly, so it becomes a sort of family joke, in itself creates a sense that their relationship is ongoing and intimate. This is the "our song" phenomenon: the existence of a shared history and shared associations both attests to and enhances intimacy. That's why it is painful to hear the words or the song after the person or the relationship is gone: It reminds us that the intimacy is gone, like a sound hanging in the air with no one to hear it. In a sense a language has died: the private language that two people created and used.

The Aesthetic Pleasure of Indirectness

Joking and other forms of irony are common and satisfying because the feat of sending and getting unstated meaning is itself aesthetically pleasing—a kind of conversational "Look,

Ma, no hands." It is a strange and compelling aspect of being human that when we get good at something we want to do it in ever more complicated and artful ways, like doing more dives, weaving more intricate designs, building more sophisticated computers, taking more elaborate photographs. How dull simply to say what is on our minds in so many words. How much more interesting to say it in a way that is funny or cryptic or subtle or stylized. And if someone else understands the humor, the style, the implications—breaks the code—it is pleasurable for both and sends a metamessage of rapport. The speaker feels clever for having pitched a curve ball, the hearer for having caught it. But if the curve is not caught—if it hits someone in the head or flies out of the ball park—no one is happy. The communication ball game is temporarily brought to a halt.

PART II:
WHY WE *CAN'T* SAY WHAT WE MEAN

If our attempts to communicate by indirectness keep tripping us up and sending us sprawling, why do we keep trying? Why don't we just say what we mean—directly?

We've seen that it's more satisfying to communicate indirectly; it would be boring simply to say what we mean, and we'd lose the metamessage of rapport. It's useful to cover ourselves by not going on record with what we think. But even if we wanted to be direct, we couldn't, for the following reasons:

First, deciding to tell the truth leaves open the question, which of the infinite aspects of the truth to tell. Second, being direct isn't enough because countless assumptions underlie anything we say or hear. We don't think of stating them precisely because they *are* assumptions. Third, stating just what we mean would often be hurtful to others. And finally, differing styles make honesty opaque. Saying what we mean in our natural style conveys something different to those whose styles differ. Attempts to get others to communicate in a way that seems natural to us will seem manipulative to them—and won't work. Let's look at examples of why we can't say what we mean.

Which Truth?

Ellen returned to her hometown for her sister's wedding. At the reception, she talked to a lot of relatives and old high-school friends. She told no untruths and had no intention of telling any, yet she gave different people very different accounts of her life as a graduate student. And she walked away from some conversations feeling she had misrepresented herself.

In some conversations, Ellen stressed how well she was doing: She liked the city she lived in, the courses she was taking, the new friends she had made. She expressed satisfaction with her life and herself and painted a rosy picture of them. But in talking to other people, Ellen painted a different picture. She stressed the negative aspects of her life: the danger and discomforts of living in a big city and in a dark and cramped apartment, the long hours of study, and the lack of free time and money.

Both pictures were true. That is, they were both composites assembled from pieces of truth. Yet both were untrue, insofar as they omitted the pieces included in the other account, as well as innumerable pieces included in neither. There is no way that Ellen, or anyone, could tell every aspect of the truth. When constructing a story for a specific occasion, we instinctively identify a main point or goal and include the details that contribute to it.

Although she didn't consciously decide to do so, Ellen painted a positive picture of her life when she spoke to relatives and her parents' friends. She didn't want them to worry about her or repeat to her parents anything that might cause them concern. The negative view of her life was constructed for her old friends from high school—women her age who were married and bored and slightly envious of her life of independence and intellectual stimulation. She wanted, instinctively, to forestall rather than incite their envy.

There is not world enough or time to state every detail, every aspect of the truth, even if we could keep them all in our minds—which we can't. Selecting words to speak and information to give always entails choices among vast alternatives. The accrual of the details that are chosen presents some aspects of the truth, inevitably falsifying or omitting others. It is impossible to tell the whole truth.

Directness Is Not Enough

A part of the truth that is necessarily left unsaid is our assumptions—aspects of the truth we do not think of saying and that, more often than not, others don't think of asking about.

A man arrived at an international airport carrying no luggage and a briefcase filled with sheets of paper covered with odd symbols and uninterpretable sentences. The customs authorities began to question him: Where would he be staying? He said he didn't know. What did he have in his briefcase? Handouts. The authorities detained him for a considerable time before they were satisfied that he wasn't up to any funny business.

Telling the authorities the truth and nothing but the truth did not get this traveler out of trouble; it got him into it. He did not announce, unasked, that he was a professor at an American university invited to deliver a lecture at a local one, so he'd be staying only one night (hence no luggage). He didn't explain that the sheets of paper that seemed to be covered with code contained sample sentences and linguistic symbols that made no sense on their own or to the uninitiate but would serve as illustrations of his lecture. When he said, truthfully, that he didn't know where he would be staying, he did not add that he would be the guest of the local university, and that reservations had been made on his behalf. Nor did he add that one of their faculty was at that moment waiting for him outside customs.

Answering directly the questions put to him was not enough because the officials didn't know enough about the situation to know what to ask. By not offering relevant information on his own, the professor gave the impression that he was hiding something. And yet he was not being dishonest; he simply neglected to state some things that were obvious to him—but not to them.

Thus, one reason we can't solve the problems of indirectness by being direct is that there are always unstated assumptions—both the speaker's and the hearer's—that may not match. We don't state them precisely because they are assumptions—by definition, ideas that are not stated because they are taken for granted. We don't become aware of assumptions until there is unmistakable evidence that they are not shared.

A very simple example of this arose when Ross called Claire and invited her for dinner.

> Ross: Why don't you come here for dinner?
> Claire: Okay. But I can't bring anything. I can only bring what I can pay for by check.
> Ross: That's a flimsy excuse!
> Claire: I can get something at the Co-op.
> Ross: But that's out of your way.
> Claire: No, it's not. I mean the one near you.
> Ross: Never mind. Just come.
> Claire: It'll just take me ten minutes to walk to the parking lot; then I'll leave.
> Ross: Oh, you have the car? I thought you were walking.

Claire: Yes, I have the car.

Ross: It's Twenty-two twenty-two Regent Street.

Claire: *What's* Twenty-two twenty-two Regent Street?!

Ross: John's house. That's where I am.

Claire: Oh, I thought you were home.

As the conversation proceeded, each one kept hearing the other say things that were surprising and odd because Claire assumed that Ross was calling from his own home, and he assumed that he was calling from John's. He forgot to state where he was, and she didn't think of asking because she assumed she knew. Neither one came out and said, "WHAT ARE YOU TALKING ABOUT?" They kept dismissing the oddness or devising interpretations for it until Claire heard something she couldn't interpret at all: Twenty-two twenty-two Regent Street.

Since we are all walking through life on an individual path, there are many times when information assumed by one is unimagined by the other. If the assumptions turn out not to be shared, we may later be blamed—and blame ourselves—for not having stated them. The right to remain silent is of no use in conversation. But it is neither natural nor possible to state all the assumptions underlying everything we say. And when problems arise, we often can't trace them back to the specific conversations, let alone the assumptions underlying them, that led us astray.

When Honesty Is Unkind

"Honesty" can result in or mask insensitivity to others' feelings. This is obvious in cases of volunteering or repeating criticism or other damaging information—a practice that is discussed at length in Chapter Nine. But it is also a danger in frequent unavoidable daily conversations about wishes and plans.

For example, Ruth makes a business trip to Houston, where her friend Emma lives. She arranges to spend an extra evening in town with her. But both Emma and Ruth end up feeling frustrated because instead of their old one-on-one intimacy, they find themselves at a group dinner including Emma's husband and another friend.

Now it happens that Emma's husband was in the middle of writing a report which he had had to leave unfinished in order to join them for dinner. Aha, you think. Emma should have been *honest*. She should have told him that she wanted to be alone with Ruth, and he would have been happy to keep working on his report.

But it's not so simple. Even though he had work to do, he *would* have been hurt to be told he wasn't wanted. Would you be happy that your best friends didn't invite you to their party, just because you happen to have other plans for that evening? Whether or not you have other plans is one thing—your thing, a matter of the message. Whether or not they invite you is another thing—a metamessage about their feelings for you.

What if Emma tried to put the metamessage into the message by saying "I love you, and I love your company, but I want to talk to Ruth alone." This would work in some cases—but only in those cases in which both people subscribe to a new system and expect such metamessages to be articulated. This system works not because it's direct but because it's shared. There is a metamessage of rapport in using a special system to which you both subscribe: "We speak the same language." In this case there's also the pleasure of using the rule of breaking rules, which sends the metamessage "We are so close, we don't have to stand on ceremony. We can say things to each other that most people wouldn't say."

But such a method will not work at all with someone who has not adopted this new style, because people believe metamessages more than messages. If Emma's husband finds it hurtful to be told that Emma doesn't want him to join them, he won't be consoled by her protest, "But I love you." He may even hear all sorts of other implications—for example, that she wants to talk about him, or that she doesn't trust his social skills.

Differing Styles Make Honesty Opaque

Part of the reason it was hard for Emma and Ruth to arrange to spend an evening alone was that the evening was a weekend—a Friday night. Ruth had wanted to spend Thursday night with Emma, but she ended up spending Friday night. The way she got into that situation was also the result of style differences.

Ruth had gotten a phone call from Albert, who also lives in Houston, and she mentioned to him that she had business in Houston on Thursday. Albert said, "Great! Let's have dinner Thursday evening. I'll keep Thursday evening free!" Ruth felt a tightness in her chest—a sign that things were going in a way she didn't want—but she began instinctively to adjust her plans to accommodate this new development. She could see Emma on Friday night.

Why didn't Ruth just say no to Albert? She wasn't prepared to deflect his offer because his way of making it was unexpected to her. Ruth expected him to make a vague offer like "Do you think you'll have time to get together?" Then she would have replied, "I hope so—maybe for lunch Thursday or Friday. I'll let you know how things go."

Who's Manipulative?

Ruth felt manipulated into having dinner Thursday night with Albert. Yet he had no intention of bullying her; he was simply showing his enthusiasm. Albert assumed that her business commitments would occupy her only during the day, and she would be free, if not casting about, for dinner. He would be hurt and puzzled to learn that she didn't really want to spend the evening with him. And he wouldn't understand why she didn't just say so. Their different styles made it hard for her to say what she meant in response to the way he said what he meant.

The feeling of being manipulated is a common result of differences in styles. For example, Ruth was supposed to pick up theater tickets for herself and Pam. But the only remaining seats were in the back, and Ruth has poor eyesight, so she needs to sit up close. She called Pam and presented the problem to her. Pam, knowing about Ruth's poor eyesight, said the obvious: that Ruth shouldn't get the tickets. But she felt manipulated. Why did Ruth make her draw the conclusion—take the role of the "heavy"—instead of telling her straight out that she wasn't getting the tickets because she wouldn't be able to see from the back? That's what Pam would have done.

Yet when Pam expressed her annoyance, Ruth felt manipulated in her turn. Why was Pam trying to force her to appear selfish and rejecting when it was obviously kinder to both of them for Ruth to let Pam back out of her own accord, instead of presenting her with a *fait accompli*?

Those who do not expect or like directness are not so much unwilling as unable to use it. For example, having been turned down twice, Burt was confused about whether or not to invite Minerva to lunch a third time. He tried to clear things up by asking, "Do you really mean you can't, or are you trying to tell me you don't want to have lunch with me so I shouldn't ask again?" Even though it was true, Minerva could not bring herself to say, "I don't want to have lunch with *you—ever*!" So she said, "Oh, well, sure, you know, it's really a busy time for me," and laughed nervously—and became more confirmed in her determination not to spend time with Burt, because he made her uncomfortable. She was turning him down indirectly because it seemed to her the only decent way to do it; she couldn't bring herself to do it any other way.

To the extent that Burt senses that Minerva expects him to back off without being explicitly told to do so, he feels manipulated. When he asks her directly whether or not she wants to have lunch with him, he is trying to circumvent her manipulativeness. But this makes her feel manipulated, because he is trying to get her to talk in a way that to her seems rude and wrong. Each feels manipulated by the other, but they're both just trying to get comfortable—and to do things right.

This is analogous to what happens when two people who are standing and talking have different ideas about how close to stand when they talk. Both try instinctively to adjust the space between them to what is natural and comfortable, with the result that one keeps backing up and the other keeps advancing. They end up edging their way down the hall. Each one feels maneuvered by the other—and is. But neither consciously intends to force the other into anything. They're both just trying to make the situation feel right. The danger—and inaccuracy—of a term like "manipulative" is that it blames others for the way we feel in response to them.

The Uses of Indirectness

Why can't we just say what we mean? Why is so much communication indirect, hinted at in metamessages, picked up in tones of voice and glimpsed in facial expressions instead of confronted head on and clearly stated in words?

First, there is a payoff in rapport. It is far better to get what we want, to be understood, without saying what we mean. It makes us feel the fine pleasure of being on the same wave length. This is the pleasure of those magical conversations when we say just a few words—or no words at all—and feel completely understood. It's the communication jackpot, the pursuit of which makes us play the birthday-present and related do-you-love-me games.

Second, there is a payoff in self-defense. If what we want or think does not meet with a positive response, we can take it back, or claim—perhaps sincerely—that that's not what we meant.

The payoffs of indirectness in rapport and self-defense correspond to the two basic dynamics that motivate communication: the coexisting and conflicting human needs for involvement and independence. Since any show of involvement is a threat to independence, and any show of independence is a threat to involvement, indirectness is the life raft of communication, a way to float on top of a situation instead of plunging in with nose pinched and coming up blinking.

Through indirectness, we give others an idea of what we have in mind, testing the interactional waters before committing too much—a natural way of balancing our needs with the needs of others. Rather than blurt out ideas and let them fall where they may, we send out feelers, get a sense of others' ideas and their potential reactions to ours, and shape our thoughts as we go.

The beauty and pitfalls of language are two sides of the same coin. A word spoken, a small gesture, can have meaning far beyond its literal sense. But subtle signals can be missed, and meaning can be gleaned that wasn't intended and that may or may not be valid. Our power to communicate so much by so few words inevitably entails the danger of miscommunication.

If others respond oddly to things we say, we may wish to try stating our intentions more directly in some situations. And knowing that others are often indirect, or for reasons of conversational style may not mean what we heard them say, we may, in some situations and with some others, ask for clarification. But we must realize that some people will feel challenged if their meaning is questioned, and any attempt to talk about ways of talking will make some people uncomfortable. So the most important thing is simply to bear in mind that the occurrence of misunderstandings is natural and normal, not a sign that there's something wrong with someone, or with the relationship.

Another way linguistic signals and devices send metamessages that communicate indirectly is by providing a frame for what we say. That is the topic of the next chapter.

CHAPTER FIVE

Framing and Reframing

Raised voices at the next table let you know that a fight is brewing. You are surprised to hear, seconds later, a burst of laughter. What you took for a fight was actually robust conversation.

You slap your friend on the back, or give him a poke, and somehow he knows you are feeling friendly toward him, not angry. But when Uncle Charlie pinches Little Butch lovingly on the cheek, it hurts, and Butch conceives a determined dislike for Uncle Charlie

Maria makes a remark about Gordon's poor taste in ties; he looks hurt and protests that several people specifically complimented him on it. Maria laughs, gives him an affectionate push and says, "Can't you take a joke?"

These fleeting understandings and misunderstandings are a matter of *framing*—another term and concept developed by Gregory Bateson. Framing is a way of showing how we mean what we say or do and figuring out how others mean what they say or do. It is another aspect of indirectness in conversation. Signals and devices like those presented in

Chapter Three serve to frame our utterances through meta-messages about what we think is going on, what we're doing when we say something, and our attitudes toward what we say and the people we say it to.

This chapter illustrates the process of framing on the various levels of conversation. Subtle signals like pitch, tone of voice, intonation, and facial expression work, along with the words we say, to frame each utterance as serious, joking, teasing, angry, polite, rude, ironic, and so on. These small, passing frames reflect and create the larger frames that identify the activities going on. For example, utterances framed as giving information contribute to the framing of a larger activity, "teaching." Teasing and complimenting can be part of a larger frame, "courting." And giving advice can be part of being protective. Everything about the way we say something contributes to establishing the footing that frames our relationships to each other.

Framing can be done only indirectly, through meta-messages. If you try to name a frame, you indirectly invoke a different one. Sometimes we feel put down by others' apparent kindness because their concern entails a subtle and unflattering reframing of our worlds. When stated and perceived frames conflict, we feel hamstrung, caught in what Bateson called a double bind. To deal with reframing that makes us uncomfortable, we can tackle the problem directly, by meta-communicating, or indirectly, by counter-reframing. Many of us instinctively stay in the frames set by others; some of us instinctively resist them. The best approach is to recognize when we feel reframed, and accept or resist it according to the situation.

Let's look more closely at these aspects of framing.

What's a Frame?

The following example of different styles of indirectness—which will sound very familiar now—also illustrates framing.

Monica asks Jay, "Where should we go for dinner?" He names a restaurant; they go there; the food is terrible. Monica mumbles, disgruntled, "It was terrible when I had lunch here with Sondra too." Jay feels tricked: "Why didn't you say so?" She is self-righteous: "You didn't ask me." And she goes on to accuse him: "You don't care what I want. We always do what you want anyway."

To Jay, it seems that Monica never says what she wants and then gets angry when she doesn't get it. What is he supposed to be, a mind reader? He can't imagine that she knows what she wants but is reluctant to impose it on him without first getting a sense of what he wants. When she asks where they should go for dinner, she expects him to respond vaguely (for example, "What are you in the mood for?") and turn the question back on her. She might then counter with something slightly less vague: "Nothing too heavy" or "I had a late lunch." Asking where he would like to go is a way to start a negotiation in which they both indicate what they would like and how strongly they feel about it, so they can agree on something that will satisfy both. But instead of a negotiation, she hears a demand from Jay about what he wants.

For her part, Monica can't imagine that when Jay names a restaurant he's just throwing out an idea—his way of starting a negotiation. He intends the restaurant he mentions as a suggestion, not a demand. Since she expects a negotiation to start vague and work its way in, and he expects it to start specific and work its way out, she never gets a chance to say what she wants and blames him for not caring, and he thinks she doesn't know or won't say what she wants and is always forcing him to decide.

When Monica asks, "Where would you like to go for dinner?" she doesn't wave a flag that says QUESTION: STEP ONE IN NEGOTIATION. When Jay throws out the name of a restaurant, he doesn't hold up a banner that says SUGGESTION: STEP ONE IN NEGOTIATION. Yet that is how they mean what they say—how they're framing their talk. Our words don't come with INSTRUCTIONS FOR USE. We don't label our utterances with the name of the frame. If we tried to, we'd have a paragraph of framing for every word of talk—and we'd need to frame the framing as such, in infinite regress.

Frames Go Nameless

Since framing, by its very nature, is signaled indirectly, naming the frame invokes a different frame. If a parent says to an adolescent son, "I'd like to have a little chat with you," he may respond, "What did I do now?" He expects something far weightier than a "little chat," which can only come about by the way, when it's not labeled. If you have to state "I'm talking to you" or "I'm trying to explain," you are probably no longer just talking or explaining but have advanced to a state of exasperation. When all is well, frames do their work unnoticed and unnamed.

If you try to get others to name their frames by asking them how they meant what they said, or what they think they're doing by saying it, they are likely to hear your question as a challenge or a criticism. They may offer a counterchallenge: "What do you *mean* what do I mean?!" Because we expect communication to proceed on its own steam, calling intentions into question in itself sends a troubling metamessage of lack of rapport.

For the most part, speakers and hearers agree, more or less, on how they're framing their conversation. For example, Shirley and Eric are talking on the phone. Suddenly Eric snaps, "Stop it!" Shirley isn't offended; she realizes that he is addressing not her but his dog, even though she can't see where he's looking. She can hear where his voice is looking in the way he speaks. There isn't time or need for Eric to say, "Wait a minute. I'm going to interrupt my conversation with you to address my dog, who has just begun to make a dinner of the carpet."

Unlike humans, dogs can identify frames only by tone of voice and other nonverbal signals, not by the meaning of words spoken. This led Eric's dog to a confusion in frames. Having correctly surmised that Eric was talking to his dog, Shirley remarked that she was surprised to hear him address the dog with a Southern accent. Eric said he always used that accent when he spoke to the dog, and he demonstrated further: "Like I say to him, 'Go git that ball!'" The dog, however, still in earshot, could not understand the words "I say to him," and therefore missed the framing of this as a quote: "*Illustrating* what I say to the dog when I want to play with him." Instead, the dog took what he heard as an invitation to play and began dashing about the room looking for something to fetch. (He settled on a stuffed frog.)

There are situations in which humans also have trouble identifying frames. One such situation is in writing. In writing, we can't use conversational signals, so we have to label or somehow flag our shifts in frames—with section headings, transition phrases, and introductory words like "In summary" or "To begin." We don't need those frame labels in speaking because we identify frame switches orally by our voice quality. That's why, when reading a transcript of conversation, it is difficult to determine how something was meant. (This has significant implications for legal proceedings which depend on a "verbatim" record of testimony or transcripts of recordings of conversation as evidence.)

If we compose speech in our heads and then write the words we would have spoken, all the elements of voice quality (pitch, timing, intonation) are lost—and so may be the frame that lets others know how we mean what we say. That's why letters are often misinterpreted. The meaning of the words is clear but a reader often misses the attitude of the writer to that meaning and toward the person addressed: Is it quizzical, affectionate, annoyed, teasing?

A professor was grading an assignment written by a particularly good student, one with whom she had a friendly relationship. The professor had made much, in class, of the necessity of limiting assignments to the number of pages allowed. The student had kept to the page limit, but she had squeezed in a lot of words by printing her assignment on a word processor that had tiny print. The professor teased the student in her written comments: "Using the word processor is a kind of cheating." The student lost a night's sleep, feeling she had seriously been accused of cheating. Had the professor made her remark in person, the student would have seen by the professor's smile and friendly manner that the accusation was teasing, not serious.

When something significant is at stake, many people prefer to discuss things on the phone rather than write about it, and would rather talk in person than on the phone. They sense that when it's important to make clear how you mean what you say, you have a better chance of doing so if you can frame your meaning with voice quality, and a still better chance if you also have nonverbal signals such as facial expression, gestures, and posture working to frame meaning as well.

When a radio station tests its emergency warning system, it has to frame the noise very explicitly: "This is a test. This is only a test." The danger of audiences' missing the frame was seen when Orson Welles read H. G. Wells's "The War of the Worlds" on the radio. Many listeners who tuned in late believed they were hearing an announcement of the real end of the world. If they had picked up a book and turned to the middle, they wouldn't have been frightened because the book physically frames its words as fiction. Radio depends on talk alone for framing.

Sometimes readers miss explicit framing even in print. A man who was unused to reading *The New York Times* picked up a copy in a friend's house. He looked up from his reading with a veil of panic across his face and said, "This is an upsetting paper to read." It turned out he had read a prediction of the imminent end of the world—and hadn't noticed that the page was framed by a box and the words PAID ADVERTISEMENT discreetly displayed in the corner.

Exploiting Frames: Ads and Jokes

Advertisers regularly make use of our framing habits. Patent-medicine ads on television used to feature men in white coats reporting laudatory information about products. The white coat, serious demeanor, and sober tone of voice framed the man as a doctor and the information he gave as scientifically sound, without the ad's saying either. Modern advertisers have become more sophisticated; it is no longer common to see actors posing as doctors in white coats, but similar framing effects are achieved by authoritative sounding voices, or by actors appearing casual, warm, and friendly, talking in tones that imply they are taking the audience into their confidence.

Many jokes depend for their effect on our framing habits by suggesting one line of interpretation, then suddenly switching frames at the end. For example, the one about the man who appears in town carrying a whip and offers to take travelers to the next town for half the usual fare. A group forms; they pay their fares and follow him, assuming he has left his horse and wagon around the corner. As they round the corner—and the next—they figure he's left his wagon at the outskirts of town. Leaving town, they conclude his wagon must be at the first way station. Well on their way to the next town—on foot—they protest: Where are his horse and wagon? "Who said anything about a wagon?" he asks. "I said I'd take you to the next town, and I'm taking you." He didn't have to say anything about a horse and wagon. The whip did the framing for him. And in hearing the joke, listeners have to switch frames at the end, revising their interpretation of the meaning of "take." Executing such a frame shift is what is thought of as "getting" a joke.

Jokes, advertisements, and con games intentionally make use of our framing habits. But because framing is done indirectly rather than explicitly, our talk can be misinterpreted when we don't intend to mislead. Like other forms of indirectness, framing constitutes both the armor and the soft underbelly of communication.

Frames in Public: I'm Working, I'm Off Duty

Differences in conventional ways of framing can cause confusion and misinterpretation in public settings. For example, "mainstream" American conventions require workers to look busy even if they aren't, but some cultural styles require people to look "cool"—that is, not busy—even if they are. A customer walks into a post office and is pleased to see that there are no other customers before her, and the clerk isn't busy. He's singing to himself, dancing in place, and dawdling with some papers, moving slowly and casually, showing no signs of focused attention. So the customer is annoyed when the clerk makes no move to help her or even to acknowledge her approach.

But the clerk really was doing something important. When he finished, he turned to her and cheerfully served her. If he had displayed toward his task an air of great attention and preoccupation, with focused movements, she would have gotten the metamessage "I'm busy" before she approached and wouldn't have expected immediate service. (In fact, he could just as easily have used these signals to give the impression of being busy when he wasn't.)

Footing

Anne was expecting an important piece of express mail on the day a severe snowstorm paralyzed the city. The next day she called the post office and asked whether she had any chance of getting her express mail. The man who answered the telephone said, "No, ma'am!" She asked, "Isn't there going to be any delivery of express mail?" He said, peremptorily and with a derisive laugh, "No, ma'am! Whatever is here is going to stay here and whatever isn't isn't. Nothing's coming in or out." His tone was saying that this was obvious. She was getting annoyed. "Well, couldn't I come and get it?" "No!" he snapped, his annoyance reaching a peak. "The post office is closed. The only reason I'm here is because I couldn't get home last night." At that Anne's frustration melted. She said, "Oh, I'm sorry. It's nice of you to answer the phone."

When Anne heard someone answer the phone, her frame was established: "open for business." But for the stranded postal worker the obvious frame was "off duty." Telling her that he couldn't get home the night before not only clued Anne in on his frame but also changed the footing on which he was talking to her—from "uncooperative employee" to "person to person."

Footing is a term used by sociologist Erving Goffman to refer to a kind of frame that identifies the relationship between speakers. The same information can be communicated with different footings—and radically different effects. Imagine a man who insists he cannot let you into the swimming pool without your card, saying, "How do I know you're not trying to sneak in?" Imagine the difference in effect if he says, "I wish I could let you in. I don't think the policy makes sense either, but I can't go against policy." In the latter instance, the footing between the card checker and client is "you and me against the system." In the first, it's "me and the system against you."

Frame changes like this can make things better—or worse. A university professor turned up at the field house of the university where she teaches and discovered that she didn't have her identification card. The student attendant at the entrance insisted she couldn't enter without it. She explained that she was on the faculty, that she swam regularly, and that her colleague, another faculty member who was with her, could identify her. The student maintained that she had better look again for her card because he couldn't let her in without it.

The professor searched in vain through her purse. Finally she pointed out that she had forgotten her card once before, and the attendant had simply entered her number into the computer. The young man said that he was also going to do that, but if he made her search for her card first, she would think twice before forgetting it again. This changed the frame from "doing my job" to "teaching you a lesson." Given the role differences, this frame puts the student on an insolent footing with respect to the professor.

The Power and Danger of Frames

The professor wrote a letter of complaint to the director of the field house. He replied that he was sure she had misinterpreted the intentions of the student who was just doing his job.

The power of frames is that they do their work off the record. By letting us mean what we say without saying what we mean in so many words, they allow us to renege, perhaps sincerely, by saying, "I didn't mean it that way," or by accusing, "What's wrong with you? You're imagining things." This defensive payoff for us as framers is a liability for us when we're uncomfortable with the frames set by others. It's far harder to challenge the way something was framed than it is to challenge a direct statement.

Most of us feel a strong impulse to sail with the framing winds. Changing course against the prevailing winds takes a great effort and risks scuttling the conversational boat. But there are two main ways to manage conversational frames rather than being blown about by them. Both ways entail changing the frame by stepping outside it. One is metacommunicating, and the other is changing the frame without talking about it.

Breaking the Frame

The best example to illustrate the drive to stay in the frame and the two ways to step outside it is a personal experience, so I'll break the frame of impersonal exposition that I've established in this book—change the footing on which I address the reader—and describe my personal experience here. (I've signaled this shift in footing explicitly because in print I can't signal it by softening my tone of voice, shifting to a more relaxed bodily stance, smiling, and so on.)

I was lecturing to a large audience. Two people sitting in the first row—a couple—were giving me trouble. They kept making derisive comments, launching long questions that challenged my assertions and derailed me from the course of my lecture. The metamessage of their comments and questions was that all I was saying was stupid and wrong.

This had never happened to me before. So I dealt with it by using the tools that had always worked in the past to reframe critical questions as not disruptive: I kept my cool; I thanked the questioners for raising interesting points, and in answering their questions, I talked about issues I wanted to address anyway. But these tools weren't sturdy enough for this reframing job because the couple didn't do their part in supporting my reframing. They didn't stop at one, two, or three questions; they called out instead of raising their hands to be recognized; they responded at length to my answers, so each question led to an extended exchange; and they tenaciously kept talking over my attempts to shorten their long responses.

As I became more unnerved by the long interruptions and challenges to my credibility, I began to make jokes at their expense. Finally, I responded to a particularly destructive challenge—the man's scornful observation that obviously people who would misunderstand each other are not very intelligent—with an impassioned, stunningly articulate and well-reasoned explication of the error of equating ways of talking with such value-laden and unfounded attributions as intelligence. Only my closest friends would have recognized my enhanced fluency and eloquence as a sign of anger. At the end of the lecture I felt like a victor following a battle: exhausted and emotionally spent, but relieved that I had prevailed.

Although I did prevail in this struggle with the contentious couple, I realized the next morning that I had not handled the situation well at all because I had stayed in the frame they had set: a battle that involved me with them as the center of attention and catapulted them out of a large audience onto center stage. Each time I responded at length to their attacks, I reinforced that frame and encouraged them to fire another round. What I should have done was break the frame, either by metacommunicating—directly talking about what was going on—or by indirectly changing it.

Metacommunicating

Metacommunicating is the term Gregory Bateson used to refer to talking about communication—naming the frame. I could have stated outright that the extended interruptions were preventing me from getting to the points I had prepared or even that I was feeling under attack. I could also have analyzed the immediate interaction in the terms of my lecture. For example, the woman had vigorously objected to my conclusion that people sometimes make impressions different from their intentions. Leaning forward out of her front-row seat, she had protested, "Surely if you're a sensitive person, you see the impression you're making, and if it's different from what you intend, then you change what you're doing!" I could have asked if she was intending right then to disrupt my lecture, appear rude, and upset me. Had she noticed that she was making that impression? Did she consider herself a sensitive person?

But calling attention to the disruptiveness of their behavior would have reinforced the battle frame by naming it and making the confrontation open. Talking about my personal reaction would have aggravated it and presented me in a more vulnerable stance than was congruent with my role as lecturer. In other words, metacommunicating changes the frame, but it also gives substance to the old frame by making it the subject of the new one, metacommunication. Metacommunicating itself carries a metamessage of involvement—like calling someone to tell him you never want to talk to him again.

Another way of stepping outside the frame would have been to say, "There are seventy-five people in this room. You've already asked a lot of questions; let's give some of the others a chance." This changes the frame without naming it.

In this way I could have reestablished control not by flexing my muscles on the specific issue ("I'm running this show and you're bugging me") but by exercising an unrelated control (giving everyone a chance to ask questions). Such a reframing would block further disruptions and dislodge this couple from the center of attention as a by-product rather than as the focus of the reframing.

Reframing in the Frame of Approval

Luck presented me with the perfect continuation of this example. The next day I had my frames changed in a very different way—in the guise of approval and support. I gave a talk to a small group of psychotherapists. Far from attacking my assertions, they enthusiastically embraced them. They took my ideas and reframed them in psychological terms: for example, "I see what you mean; he was hostile." Unfortunately, what was offered as a show of understanding was actually evidence of lack of it. My point was precisely that the behavior mistakenly seen as hostile was really a well-intentioned act in a different style.

An even more powerful type of reframing in that setting went like this. I decided to use my experience of the night before to demonstrate the concept of frames, as I have just done here. As soon as I finished explaining what had happened, and before I proceeded to analyze it, the psychotherapist sitting next to me reached out, touched my shoulder, and said, "Let's role-play that." This gesture reframed the interaction, casting me as a patient and her as my therapist!

Metacommunicating in this case would be to say, "Hey, I'm not your patient!" To resist the reframing without naming the frame would be to say, "Wait, I haven't finished talking about these examples."

It is as frustrating to be praised as to be criticized if we feel the praise is based on a frame that isn't ours—like the complaint in the song "Killing Me Softly": "telling my whole life in his words." We want to tell our own lives in our own words. And it is frustrating to be helped (as I was "helped" to role-play an interaction I had found difficult) if that help establishes a footing with which we don't feel comfortable. It's no fun being embraced if the embrace cuts off your breath.

Reframing as Put-down

Sometimes you feel put down by what others say, and you're not sure why, especially if they appear to be saying something kind.

Shortly after her divorce, Marjorie took a trip to London over the Christmas holiday. When she said good-bye to her friends Julian and Barb, Barb patted her lovingly on the arm and said with a smile, "You don't have to go all the way to London not to be alone on Christmas. Next year you can spend Christmas with us."

Marjorie said thank you for the kind offer. But she felt rotten. Her exciting trip to London was reframed as a pathetic attempt to avoid being alone on the holiday. Yet because the reframing was done by an apparently generous gesture, she didn't think of objecting. Even if she had thought of it, she wouldn't have said anything because any objection would introduce a contentious tone into the thus-far harmonious interchange.

Such a communication is confusing because it's a double bind: the message and metamessage conflict. The message says "We're your friends; we want you to be happy." The metamessage says "You poor thing," and that makes you *feel* like a poor thing—and feel correspondingly miserable.

Another time Marjorie was expecting a visit from Caroline—a friend who happened to be, like Marjorie, a successful stockbroker. When she mentioned to Sophia that Caroline would be staying at her house, Sophia said, "Oh, good, you'll have a chance to pick her brains." This reframed the friendly visit from a peer as a situation in which Marjorie was the lucky beneficiary of a visit by a superior. In this sense, it's insulting, reducing Marjorie's status. But the insult isn't in the proposition, it's in the assumptions underlying it—in other words, in the framing.

A group of friends is having dinner at a restaurant. They are in the habit of tasting each other's food, especially if it is something interesting. Karen offers Laura a taste of her roast duck, and Laura accepts. Then she offers Karen a taste of her scallops, and Karen declines, saying soothingly, "You don't have so many. You keep them."

Suddenly Laura feels like a pig because she's hogging her own dinner. Karen turned down Laura's offer in a way that framed her refusal as magnanimous, and it was made even more so because she had just given of her duck. Karen seemed to imply that she wanted to taste the scallops but would deny herself so as not to take any away from Laura. (Perhaps Karen was actually expecting Laura to offer again, more insistently.) True magnanimity would have consisted in pretending not to want any, so Laura could eat all her scallops without feeling she was depriving Karen.

Karen's magnanimity, framed by the way she declined the offer, underlies the classic "martyred mother" stance ("Don't mind me—I'll just sit here in the dark.") It's an ironic twist by which you want to be magnanimous but want credit for it too—and taking credit for being magnanimous reframes the other's behavior as depriving you. It is not necessary to see this as intentionally destructive on the part of guilt inspirers. It is sufficient that they want their magnanimity on record. The reframing of the other's behavior is a by-product of that frame.

Frame Savers and Frame Breakers

A man and a woman are walking down the street. A car approaches the intersection at the same time they do. The driver of the car stops at the corner and signals them to cross in front of him. Such apparent kindness is, in a sense, inappropriately self-aggrandizing. If there is a crosswalk, it is the law, not the driver's magnanimity, that requires him to let the pedestrians cross. By waving them across, the driver takes credit for an externally defined situation, like Karen's converting Laura's own scallops into a gift from her.

How does the couple at the corner respond to this reframing? The woman quickens her pace and hurries across the street. The man backs up and signals the driver of the car to go ahead while he waits.

The woman's instinct is to accept the frame set by the driver: "I'm allowing you to cross." She quickens her pace to return kindness for kindness by avoiding keeping the driver waiting more than necessary. The man's instinct is to resist the driver's frame and substitute his own: "No, *I'm* allowing *you* to go ahead."

Whereas it might seem as though the right to go ahead gives one the upper hand, that is only the message level. On the metamessage level, the one who *decides* who goes ahead has the upper hand, regardless of who gets to go. This is why many women do not feel empowered by such privileges as having doors held open for them. The advantage of going first through the door is less salient to them than the disadvantage of being granted the right to walk through a door by someone who is framed, by his magnanimous gesture, as the arbiter of the right-of-way.

Most of us tend either to resist or to yield to frames. Those who instinctively resist frames set by others tend to balk when they feel pushed. Those who instinctively fit inside the frames set by others tend to yield when they feel pushed. We are more likely to respond according to our habits than to the specifics of the situation.

It would be better to learn to respond one way or the other—to go with the frame or resist—depending on the situation. The first step toward this exercise of control is to recognize when we feel uncomfortable with the frames we're put in and understand the ways of talking that are doing the framing. The second is to practice ways of resisting that framing or of changing frames by talking differently. In some cases, it may even be worthwhile to metacommunicate: to talk about the frame, with or without using the term.

Frames Are Dynamic

Frames are not static, like picture frames, but are constantly evolving lines of interpretation, continually negotiated footings. The framing that is going on at any moment is part of what establishes the frame for what goes on next, and is partly created by the framing that went before. The footing we establish at any moment is occasioned by the footing that was established the moment before—and the year before.

At any point, each person is both reacting to and causing a reaction in others. Most of us tend to see ourselves as responding to what others say, without realizing that what they are saying may be a reaction to us. We are keenly aware that we said what we did because of what she said, but it may not occur to us that she said what she did because of what we said—just before, yesterday, or last year. Communication is a continuous stream in which everything is simultaneously a reaction and an instigation, an instigation and a reaction. We keep moving in a complex dance that is always different but made up of familiar steps. The constantly shifting rhythm and sequence is adjusted by subtle metamessages that frame what's going on from moment to moment.

Some of these examples of framing and reframing have to do with feeling put down or supported, manipulated or in control. This aspect of framing can be understood in terms of one last dimension of human communication—power and solidarity. And that is the subject of the next chapter.

CHAPTER SIX

Power and
Solidarity

Jack visits his grandmother in a nursing home. She boasts that she is really "in" with the nurses because they call her Millie. Jack isn't pleased; he thinks they aren't treating his grandmother with proper respect. Jack feels the nurses are establishing toward her a footing that reinforces their position of power; she takes their using her first name as an expression of solidarity.

The terms *power* and *solidarity* capture the way we juggle involvement and independence in the real world. Power has to do with controlling others—an extension of involvement—and resisting being controlled—an extension of independence: the desire not to be imposed on. But it also has to do with registering social status, because superior status entails the right to control and to resist being controlled. Solidarity is the drive to be friendly, similar to what we have called rapport, but power also establishes equal footing between people, so neither one can tell the other what to do.

It's easy to see how superior status lets us tell others what to do. Employers give orders to employees; parents to children; teachers to students; doctors to nurses and patients. But even in situations of apparently equal footing—among friends, or between partners in love or business—the needs for involvement and independence constantly invoke issues of control.

Indirectness makes it possible to control others without appearing to. The father who lets his daughter know what he thinks she should do without actually telling her wants to get his way. But he'd rather feel he's getting his way because his daughter wants the same thing (solidarity) than because he's twisting her arm (power). Thus power can masquerade as solidarity. But knowing this, we can mistake sincere expressions of solidarity for power plays and put-downs. In shaking my hand, do you give an extra squeeze to let me know you like me—or to let me know you're stronger? I may get either message, regardless of which you intend.

Power and solidarity are paradoxically related to each other; they are both mutually exclusive and mutually entailed. Love implies wanting to please the ones we love, so getting others to love us is a way of getting what we want. Thus solidarity entails power. Fear results in doing what the ones we fear want, so getting others to fear us is also a way of getting what we want—and of getting signs of love. Thus power entails solidarity.

The dimensions are further intertwined because loving always entails fear that love will be lost. So both love and fear can result in feeling (or being) controlled and controlling (or trying to control) others.

It's a paradox, like the drawing of a chalice and two faces. Both images exist in the picture simultaneously, and we can see both, but we can see only one at a time. In the same way, we can see only one side of the power/solidarity dimension at a time. If you are trying to get me to do what you want— manipulating me—then you don't love me; you're using me. It's hard to see—because it *is* contradictory—that you love me *and* you're using me. You want me to do what you want *and* you want me to be free. Such paradoxes keep communication (and relationships) in a state of imbalance and continual correction.

What's in a First Name?

The example of the woman in the nursing home is a good place to begin exploring the power/solidarity dimension because forms of address are among the most common ways of showing status and affection. Solidarity reigns when two people call each other by first name. Power reigns when one calls the other by first name but it's not reciprocal. If a man tells his servant, "When the guests arrive, show them into the drawing room, Steven," can Steven reply, "I'd be glad to, Ronald"? If a teacher calls on Johnny to read the lesson aloud, can Johnny ask, "Which page, Margaret?" If the doctor or dentist or psychotherapist calls the secretary or client "Mary," can Mary respond in kind?

Age, gender, and status all play roles here. In a sense the age relationship is a model for power and solidarity. Any adult can call any child by first name, but children must call at least some adults by title-last name (Mr., Ms., Miss, Mrs., Dr.). Ways of talking to children—calling them by first name, patting and caressing them, asking them personal questions—show affection. But they also reflect a difference in status because the right to show affection in that way is not reciprocal.

By extension, when a businessman, Mr. Warren, says to the elevator operator, "Good morning, Jimmy" he means to be friendly, but Jimmy may be thus reminded of the difference in their positions. And if Jimmy is standing in the hall talking to the janitor, Mr. Warren may touch his arm to move him aside. But Mr. Warren would expect Jimmy to stand aside and say, "Excuse me," if Jimmy wanted Mr. Warren to move aside.

Mr. Warren may also feel free to move any woman who is blocking his path by touching her in a friendly way, whereas he would refrain from physical contact and say, "Excuse me" (in other words, be more formal than friendly), if his path were blocked by another man in a three-piece suit. Someone who consciously intends to be friendly can be perceived as pulling rank if his way of being friendly is not reciprocal, or not the way he'd be friendly with a peer.

Women are often caught in the grip of this paradox. They are far more often called by their first names and touched than are men. Talk-show hosts, panel moderators, students, and others far more often address men with Ph.D.s as "Doctor" than they do women with Ph.D.s. It's common for strangers—travel agents, salespeople, telephone-order clerks—to use the first names of all women customers. In one sense, this shows condescension: lack of respect. Just as people feel free to touch, pat, and first-name children, they feel freer to use these friendly signs with women.

But the fact remains that people who treat women in this way are doing it to be friendly; using "Miss" or "Mrs." (let alone "Ms."!) would feel awkward, like anything that goes against habit. Many women prefer to be called by first name because it's distancing to be addressed by title-last name. And women are more likely than men to be troubled by distancing.

"Thanks, Honey"

A rising young executive was interviewing a prospective recruit for her firm over an informal lunch. The restaurant had a serve-yourself setup for coffee. The executive was pouring coffee for herself when a man approached and asked her to pour some for him. She obliged, gladly. He said, "Thanks, honey. I'll do the same for you sometime."

Although she hadn't objected to being asked to pour coffee

(other women might), the executive felt herself reframed as lower in status than she was by the intimate form of address. She said to the stranger, "Thanks, but don't call me honey."

This comeback made the man furious. He sputtered and spluttered and finally accused her: "I'll bet your husband calls you honey and you love it!" This, of course, was just the point. He wasn't her husband, so he shouldn't address her as her husband might. But the man had made a friendly gesture, so her taking offense seemed to him unjust. He was aware of the metamessage of solidarity in calling her "honey." She was reacting to the metamessage of condescension.

Sadly, there is no term this man could have used to show his friendly feelings without being condescending. "Pal," "mac," or "buddy" wouldn't be appropriate for a woman. All the traditional terms of affection for women have come to seem condescending precisely because they are used only with women. This is why dealing with women (or others who are different) in settings where we are used to dealing only with men is frustrating. The ways traditionally used to talk to men seem impolite, but the ways traditionally used to talk to women imply not according them the same respect a man would get.

The doctor who pats his patient or nurse on the arm, saying, "How are you today, Sally?," may genuinely intend to be warm and friendly. But because the patient or nurse couldn't pat him on the arm and ask, "How are you today, Richie?," there's a (possibly unintended) metamessage of superior status in the doctor's gesture. The ways he has of showing concern or getting close—using first name, touching, and inquiring about health—are paradoxically also expressions of superior status, which is condescending.

Many of us, faced with such mixed metamessages, either resent the condescension and ignore the concern or appreciate the concern and ignore the condescension. As in looking at a paradoxical drawing, we can't hold on to both images at once. But they're both there. Feeling either anger at the condescension or appreciation of the concern ignores half the communication.

Denying Power

Once again we see that communication is a double bind. What is a well-intentioned doctor to do? Many clients do not appreciate the invitation to call their doctor by first name because they feel there really is a difference in status—one they want to bear in mind as they entrust their lives to the doctor.

Even very young patients respond to the metamessages in how doctors talk to them. Four-year-old Ben Clarke's family doctor was hip. He went by the name Ralph and engaged his young patients in chitchat before examining them. One time Ben had to see a specialist who was more traditional and formal. After the visit Ben remarked to his father, approvingly, "Now *that's* a doctor!" When asked, Ben explained, "He talks like a doctor."

If a doctor encourages patients and nurses to call him by first name and ask him about his personal life, he may be seen as affecting false equality. If a woman doctor does this, she may sacrifice even more of the signs of respect that medical status should confer. Trying to be "just folks" when you're not can seem hypocritical and provoke resentment when authority rears its head—for example, when a doctor insists that a patient or nurse follow his instructions about medical procedures. And teachers who encourage displays of solidarity find themselves squarely in the power camp when they have to assign grades or make decisions about placement.

It is generally up to doctors, bosses, professors, and older people to grant permission to others to address them by first name or use other signs of familiarity. (Women in these positions sometimes find this prerogative usurped, as has just been explained.) The act of granting permission to take a role of equality in itself frames one as in a superior position. And those who grant permission to use some signs of equal status will certainly have strong feelings about which liberties should not be taken. A female professor who did not mind her students calling her by her first name, and employed a friendly manner rather than a professorial one, was nevertheless annoyed when a male student congratulated her on an academic honor and capped the praise by patting her on the back and chuckling—and when another responded to her request to please hand her something with a playfully teasing "Say pretty please."

Solidarity undercuts power. We can't have it both ways. The social worker who seeks to be accepted by a gang relinquishes authority. To the extent that he preserves his authority, or the right to invoke it in extreme circumstances, he cannot be accepted as an equal by the gang.

Shows of solidarity by someone perceived to be of higher status can backfire and seem condescending. The use of informality to show solidarity by one perceived to be of lower status can backfire and seem insolent. And the first case can invite the second. Status differences are expressed and maintained by ways of talking, but they can also be unintentionally invoked because ways of talking send metamessages about status, intended or not.

Reframing Along the Power/ Solidarity Dimension: Claiming Inappropriate Equality

Chapter Five presented examples of comments that cause discomfort because the speaker assumes a footing that the hearer deems inappropriate. Sometimes the inappropriateness has to do with relative status; then the power/solidarity dimension is at play. Praise, for example, isn't appreciated when it seems to set the praiser up as your superior—in a position to judge you.

A free-lance writer who is also on the faculty of a journalism school received a letter congratulating her on a feature article that appeared in a major newspaper. Following is an excerpt from that letter. Ask yourself what footing the letter writer seems to be establishing in relation to the journalist:

> I write to you after all this time because I have read your article and I was quite impressed with it. You described exactly what has affected quite a number of people in the same position, and recently I came to the same conclusion myself. Thanks for sharing your views so clearly. Too bad we never talked about this when I was in New York. It might have been quite an interesting discussion. I am convinced, after reading your article, that we hold a similar view on this topic and would have agreed on many points. Keep up the good work!

The journalist was surprised to get this letter from a former student—one much younger, who was not a writer herself. The phrasing of the praise—being "quite impressed," congratulating the writer on reaching the same conclusion that she reached, assuming the journalist would have wanted to discuss matters with the letter writer had she known that they would agree—all establish a footing which frames the praiser as in a superior position. Encouragement like "Keep up the good work!" can imply that the one cheering you on has been waiting for ages at the finish line.

When someone invokes solidarity that seems inappropriate, we resent it. Parents who try to talk or dress like their teenage children are often chided by the children for doing it all wrong. What the children may be objecting to, at heart, is that their parents are claiming membership in a group they don't really belong to—invoking unjustified solidarity.

A teenage boy played his new rock album for his father, who was a classical music fan. The father declared that this was terrific music, and he began to explain why he found it artistically admirable. Rather than being pleased, the boy was annoyed. "Can't I have anything to myself?" he asked. He wanted, in the matter of music, to feel that he was the expert and his father the outsider. He felt that by embracing his music, his father was taking it over.

In the matters of music, clothes, or ways of talking, the parents' purpose may not be to control but to feel solidarity with their children. Yet the children may experience their parents' moves to accept or emulate their behavior as a power-based invasion. And often solidarity *is* invoked in order to influence; it is not by chance that the phrases "win friends" and "influence people" are commonly joined in the same expression.

Winning Friends to Influence People: Selling

The salesman who slaps you on the back and calls you by first name may alienate rather than charm you because he's acting as if he were your friend. Not only do you feel the solidarity is inappropriate, but you sense that he's posing as your friend in order to influence you as a friend might—to buy his product. Salespeople instinctively understand the connection between solidarity and control. Priming for a sale is a matter of establishing a friendlike footing.

A salesperson who helps you select a new suit, stepping back and telling you that the suit is "really you" and makes you look like a million dollars, may be genuinely trying to see what looks best on you, as a friend would—or may be aiming at a million dollars in profit for the store.

A woman glances at a cosmetics counter. The saleswoman begins giving her friendly advice and soon is applying sample cosmetics products to the customer's face. Wiping a piece of cotton soaked with expensive liquid across the customer's forehead, the saleswoman triumphantly sticks the cotton in front of the customer's eyes: "And you thought your face was clean! Look at that!" Since it's six P.M. in a dirty city, the customer had no reason to think her face was clean. But her good manners, her impulse to preserve solidarity by not contradicting, prevent her from posing a challenge: "Who said I thought my face was clean?"

Then the saleswoman makes an offer of great intimacy: "Feel my face. Isn't that soft?" The customer's ingrained politeness does not allow her to recoil from this offer or to say anything but "Oh, yes, your skin is very soft." Another triumph for the saleswoman: "It's because I use this product!"

Having agreed that her face is dirtier than she thought, and that the woman who uses the product has very soft skin, the customer is channeled into a line of reasoning that leads to the logical conclusion of buying the product. To refuse to buy it, she must present herself as not wanting clean, soft skin. That's how salespeople make use of our conversational habits to invoke solidarity for the purpose of control.

Those hired as salespeople often are (or pretend to be) experts on the products they're selling—cosmetics, computers, or electronics equipment. But the person who comes to a store for free advice can easily be converted into a customer. Then it is open to question whether the computer salesperson will recommend the computer that best suits the customer's needs or the one that affords the highest commission.

When a salesperson shifts from answering questions to making a sale (a gradual shift, of course), it is similar to the frame change that occurs when a teacher who has been helping students learn suddenly shifts roles and grades them. Teachers are usually caught unwillingly and even unawares in this conflict of frames; the solidarity-based (but power-tinged) teaching role is the one they sought. In sales, the reverse may be true: The solidarity-based role of giving information is provided to set the stage for control: making a sale.

Invoking Inappropriate Distance

Just as solidarity can do double duty, so can distance. Standing off to be polite or considerate, including using title and last name, can be taken as a show of superiority—being uppity or snobbish. Imagine an adolescent who returns from finishing school and begins addressing family members with formally polite language. The family reaction might be "Are you angry at us?" or "Do you think you're too good for us now?" A failure of solidarity can thus be interpreted as a presumption of superiority.

Ways of talking that show politeness (intended to preserve solidarity) by giving options or keeping distance are the same ways that show deference, or inferior status. So "politeness" can come across as self-deprecating. This can double-bind people who use conventionally polite styles—for example, women and Southerners (outside the South). Their ways of building solidarity give the impression they feel powerless: unassertive and wishy-washy. Such styles may succeed in making others like them, but may not get them promoted.

Other kinds of self-deprecation do not make one likable. A famous speaker appears at a conference only long enough to deliver a lecture, after which he disappears. His colleagues murmur about how he thinks he's too important to waste time listening to other speakers. Actually he escapes quickly from the conference because social interaction with those he doesn't know well is painful for him. Not knowing how to approach others, he stands aside and averts his glance, giving the impression of being unapproachable. Then he feels hurt when no one talks to him. What is perceived as a display of power is really a failure of solidarity. Far from feeling too good for everyone, he feels not good enough.

Ambition

The presumption of power motives when solidarity may be involved is relevant to an understanding of ambition, a quality about which our society is ambivalent. Ambition is the expression of desire for both power and solidarity. But we tend to see ambition as only power-based.

One goal of ambition is to exercise control over others: to get our way, to know that our word will stick. But another goal of ambition is to be loved: to know that we won't be ignored, that our word will be heard. The effects of these two goals may be the same, but the motivations are different.

Being a politician—whether inside or outside the arena of politics per se—entails a style many of us feel is by definition insincere. But politics, like other spheres of success and influence, is a matter of both aspects of ambition. People seek political influence to feel powerful, but also to feel loved by as many others as possible.

Political skills like remembering people's names and personal details about them are simply developments of the social skills for building rapport. One commentator described the quintessential politician as someone who can "work the room," and he named Hubert Humphrey as epitomizing this skill. Humphrey would sail into a room where scores of people were seated for dinner, stop at each table, and greet all the guests in turn by name, with a reference to something personal about them.

A cynical way to view this behavior is that the politician is feigning interest to garner favor and, ultimately, votes. This view is supported by movies and TV: A politician talks on the telephone as his assistant hurriedly finds and hands him a card. Grabbing it, the politician bellows into the phone, "Great talking to you! My best to Mary and little Jennifer! Great! Great!"

But this exuberance can as easily be sincere. The model for such manipulation is the person who spontaneously pleases others by remembering their names and details about them—and really enjoys making personal, though fleeting, contact with a vast number of people. Any behavior that can be feigned is effective because some people display it naturally. Ambitious people may be motivated by different mixtures of desire for power and solidarity.

Power and Solidarity at Home

The paradoxical frames of power and solidarity explain a lot of our interpersonal struggles. As an example, let's consider an amusing but not unusual conversation that was taped by someone who happened to be there and later analyzed by one of the first professional conversational analysts, sociologist Harvey Sacks. A transcript of the conversation follows. It took place at Bill's home. Ethel and Ben are Bill's parents, and Max is their stepfather-in-law. Ethel and Ben are trying to get Max to eat some herring, and Max refuses.

> Ben: You have to . . . uh . . . uh—Hey, this is the best herring you ever tasted. I'll tell you that right now.
> Ethel: Bring some out so that Max could have some too.
> Ben: Oh, boy.
> Max: I don't want any.
> Ben: They don't have this at Mayfair, but this is delicious.
> Ethel: What's the name of it?
> Ben: It's the Lasko but there's herring snack bits and there's reasons why—the guy told me once before that it was the best. It's Nova Scotia herring.
> Bill: Why is it the best?
> Ben: 'Cause it comes from cold water. 'Cause cold-water fish is always
> Max: [?] when they . . . uh . . . can it.
> Ethel: Mmmm.

Ben: Cold-water fish is—

Ethel: Ooooo, Max, have a piece.

Ben: This is the best you ever tasted.

Ethel: Geschmacht. Mmm. Oh, it's delicious. Ben, could you hand me a napkin, please.

Bill: Lemme cut up a little piece a' bread.

Ben: Innat good?

Ethel: Delicious. Geschmacht, Max.

Max: What?

Ethel: Geschmacht. Max, one piece.

Max: I don' want.

Ben: You're gonna be—You better eat sump'n because you're gonna be hungry before we get there.

Max: So?

Ben: C'mon. Here. I don't wancha to get sick.

Max: Get there I'll have something.

Ben: Huh?

Max: When I get there I'll eat.

Ben: Yeah, but you better eat something before. You wanna lay down 'n take a nap?

Max: No.

Ben: C'mon. You wanna sit up and take a nap? Cause *I'm* gonna take one.

Max: [?]

Ben: —in a minute. That's good. That is really good.

Ethel: Mmm.

Ben: Honestly. C'mon.

Max: I don't [?]

Ben: [?] Please, I don't wancha to get sick.

Max: I don't get sick.

Ben: Ooo, that's so—

Ethel: It's just sorta—

Ben: Innat—Innat—

Ethel: —tickles the tongue, doesn't it?

Ben: Mhm. Maybe we oughta take one—take one home with us.

Bill: Where dju get it.

Ethel: Alpha Beta [up here].
 Bill: Right here?
Ethel: Mmhm.
 Bill: Hm.
Ethel: Hm—you better put some more in the dish, Ben.
   Would you be good enough to empty this in there
   and then I'll fill it *up* for you again.
 Ben: Yeah I know.
Ethel: Thank you.
 Ben: Max doesn't know what he's missing.
 Bill: *He* knows.
 Ben: I don' want him to get sick. I want him to eat.

In his analysis, Sacks explains that Max's wife recently died. So Ethel and Ben feel responsible for him, and they consider their responsibility to include making sure Max eats. If his wife were alive and present, it would be her job to make him eat—or not eat.

As Max turns down the offers of food, he becomes a stubborn old man in their eyes. As Sacks put it, "You can imagine that he ages in the re-offering, and they say, 'Oh my God, it's that old man sitting there not eating anything, he's going to get sick for sure.'" But from Max's point of view, "For 35 years people have been telling him what to eat and when to eat, and now that he doesn't have a wife to tell him what to eat, he'll damn well eat what he wants. But as soon as he happens to be in that position, then somebody else figures 'My God, he's all by himself, somebody has to watch out for him.'" Whereas *they* see "he's being obstinate for no good reason," *he* sees he has to "get them to recognize that they can't force him to do things, or he's going to be turned into their little boy."

What for Ethel and Ben is framed as solidarity—taking care of Max—is for him a show of power—treating him like a little boy. What for him is an exercise of independence—"I can eat what I want"—is for them a failure of involvement—

he has no one to take care of him. They all stay within their own frames, so together they are caught in a spiraling frame of a battle of wills.

A Juggling Act

In this conversation as in all human communication, overriding other considerations are the coexisting and conflicting needs for independence and involvement, partly expressed in the balancing of power and solidarity. Among Ethel, Ben, and Max, the issue isn't herring, but caring and independence, love and freedom.

In all our communication, we struggle to maintain our independence, to resist being controlled by others, without jeopardizing our involvement or losing their love. And we strain to show love—honoring needs to be involved and to have others want what we want or at least approve of what we want—without engulfing them or being engulfed, in other words, without having solidarity shade into power.

The same ways of talking can imply solidarity or a power differential. A show of solidarity to honor involvement can seem like an imposition (a violation of independence), condescension (insincere solidarity), or insolence (claiming inappropriate equality). On the other hand, the same ways of talking that show politeness by deference (not imposing) can seem ineffectual (lacking in power), snobbish (pretending to be superior), or pulling rank.

The dimensions and processes of conversation that have been described thus far are operating in all communication: Conversational signals and devices send metamessages about involvement and independence that work indirectly to frame our talk and express and negotiate our relationships to each other, including juggling the relative power and solidarity entailed in those relationships. These processes operate in all conversations, but they are seen especially clearly, and their effects are especially frustrating, in conversations that take place over time, at home. The next section of this book shows how these processes of conversational style are played out in relationships among intimates: family members and romantic partners.

Talking at Home: Conversational Style in Close Relationships

CHAPTER SEVEN

Why Things Get Worse

It was the question period following one of my lectures about conversational style, a lecture about indirectness, misreading of intentions, tempers flaring over small matters like where to go for dinner and whether or not to go to a party. A woman sitting in the back of the audience raised her hand and said: "When my boyfriend and I first went out, we never had any problems like that. Now we've been together for two years, and we have them all the time. How come?!" This is one of the great puzzles of close relationships: WHY DO THINGS OFTEN GET WORSE INSTEAD OF BETTER?

Things may seem to get worse in close relationships that continue over time because we don't realize that communication is inherently ambiguous and that conversational styles differ, so we expect to be understood if there is love. When misunderstandings inevitably arise, we attribute difficulties to failure: our own, or the other's, or a failure of love.

The more contact people have with each other, the more opportunities both have to do things in their own way and be misunderstood. The only way they know of to solve problems is to talk things out, but if different ways of talking are causing a problem, talking more isn't likely to solve it. Instead, trying harder usually means doing more of whatever you're doing—intensifying the style that is causing the other to react. So each unintentionally drives the other to do more and more of the opposing behavior, in a spiral that drives them both up the wall.

Part of the reason this mutual aggravation of style differences is so disturbing is that we want so badly for communication to be perfect at home. Primary relationships have replaced religion, clan, and mere survival as the foundations of our lives, and many of us (especially but not only women) have come to see communication as the cornerstone of that foundation.

To add to the problem, the worsening of communication is the opposite of what we expect. We feel toward the person we have been with for a long time: "You should understand me, if anyone does." Feeling misunderstood by this person is upsetting not because of the minor frustration of eating at the wrong restaurant or missing the party but because of the metamessage about the relationship: "If, after all this time, we still misunderstand each other, there's something wrong with our relationship." And even more distressing: "If you, to whom I have shown my realest self, don't like what you see, then my real self must be pretty awful."

All this means that the platitude "If you love each other, you can work it out" is not necessarily true. Instead, the more you love each other, the more unrealistic your expectations of perfect understanding, and the more painful the metamessage of misunderstanding. And that, in turn, is why so many people, finding that they can't work it out, conclude that they don't—or even less logically, never did—love each other.

Another way that the reality of relationships sometimes falls short of our expectations is that we expect through marriage to prolong the pleasures of courting. But in courting, you start from a position of distance and look for signs that the other person wants to get closer. Under such magnification, small signs take on great—and wonderful—meaning. In long-term relationships, you start from a position of closeness and are on the lookout for signs that the other person wants to get farther away. By the same process of magnification, you are likely to find what you're looking for.

Late in the screenplay *Scenes from a Marriage by* Ingmar Bergman, Johan and Marianne meet years after their divorce. Marianne asks, "Why are we telling the truth now? I know. It's because we make no demands." It's not that either of them has improved or matured, but simply that their situation has changed. Since they are no longer married to each other, they need less from each other, and no longer need the metamessage of perfect rapport.

Dennis observed to Jean, after they had been dating for about a year, "In the beginning I felt like I could tell you anything. Now I don't feel like I can anymore." Then he figured out why: "I guess in the beginning I could tell you anything because we had nothing to lose. Now I'm scared to cause trouble by telling you things you're not going to like." This is one of the basic reasons why things get worse. The closer you are to someone, and the longer you have been close, the more you have to lose when you open your mouth.

Getting to Know You: The Myth

Conventional wisdom and common sense tell us that the more time people spend together, the better they will understand each other. And the way to reach such understanding is honest talk. As the husband, Jake, says to his wife, Louise, in Jules Feiffer's play *Grown Ups*, "I'll say what I want to. Without interruption. You say what you want to after I finish. And it'll be over and done with." This sounds unassailably reasonable—to us as to Louise, who agrees: "O.K. When you put it that way, O.K. Go ahead." Yet two lines later, Jake and Louise are at each other's throats, and at the end of the play, they are getting a divorce.

The belief that sitting down and talking will ensure mutual understanding and solve problems is based on the assumption that we can say what we mean, and that what we say will be understood as we mean it. This is unlikely to happen if conversational styles differ. Furthermore, in saying what we mean, we often think only of the message. But listeners (including us, when we're listening to others) respond most strongly to metamessages. So our expectations of the benefits of honesty are unlikely to match the reality of communication.

These expectations and realities apply to international as well as personal relations. The concept of summit meetings among heads of state is based on the assumption that extended exposure leads to better understanding. For example *Newsweek* pointed out, "Defenders of the summit process argue that, even if they produce no substantial results, the sessions enhance understanding among the leaders."

But in world as well as private affairs, reality often flies in the face of our expectations (which remain blithely unaffected by reality). So *Newsweek* continued, "But Jimmy Carter and Helmut Schmidt saw one another at four successive summits and their mutual dislike only grew deeper."

Even if members of different cultures don't dislike each other, there is no reason to expect that they will emerge with the same interpretations of what has been said. Thus *Newsweek* added:

> At the Versailles summit last year all parties worked hard to reach face-saving compromise language on the explosive issues of East-West trade and currency intervention. But no sooner was the meeting over than American and European spokesmen gave diametrically opposed versions of what had been agreed to.

Each side probably believed that the other deliberately falsified or altered their reports of what had been agreed to. But it's likely that they had different understandings of what they were saying even at the time they agreed.

Getting to Know You: The Reality

When Ronnie and Bruce first met, each tried to be considerate of what the other wanted, and they didn't mind if they didn't get what they wanted because they were so happy to have found each other and so eager to please. If they ended up doing what neither wanted, neither one knew and both felt satisfied that they were pleasing the other. If the truth came out, they had a good laugh over it and chalked it up to the process of getting to know each other.

At beginning stages of their relationship, Ronnie and Bruce felt misunderstandings were to be expected. Being able to talk about them seemed like proof of good will and growing rapport and would certainly prevent such misunderstandings in the future. But the future became a present full of misunderstandings, and the fact that they continued to occur in itself became a source of dismay.

At the same time, living their lives as a couple, Ronnie and Bruce had to make more and more decisions taking the other's wishes into account, until life seemed like an endless series of minor negotiations. When the negotiations kept getting complicated and confusing, each tended to blame the other, not the situation or the process of communication.

As relationships continue, little frustrations pile up to a cumulative effect of big frustration. Love (contrary to conventional wisdom and popular opinion) does not preclude getting frustrated with someone. Quite the opposite, the more time two people spend together, the more opportunity they have to observe the other's behavior—and disapprove, especially when everything one does affects the other's life.

As relationships continue, if style differences cause misunderstandings, each new misunderstanding gives added evidence for negative conclusions about the other: She is unreasonable, he is uncooperative; she is inconsiderate, he is selfish; she is pushy, he is antisocial. And each new piece of evidence can be stuffed into an already bulging gunnysack of individually minor complaints.

Communicating over time sets up expectations that the other will behave in certain ways. Expecting something often makes you see it before it happens. Wanting to head off expected offenses at the pass sometimes leaves you standing alone in the road near the pass waving a sword at the air.

A Big Deal About Nothing

One of the maddening aspects of close relationships is finding yourself in fights over insignificant matters. One of the reasons small matters take on big meaning is that the context of a close relationship makes all that is said wobble under the heavy weight of a frame that surrounds everything with the question "Do you love me enough?" When the speakers have different assumptions about how to frame their talk and show their love, the resultant misunderstandings have a spiraling effect.

Here's a conversation that took place between two people who lived together and loved each other. Mike was preparing dinner for them both:

Mike: What kind of salad dressing should I make?
 Ken: Oil and vinegar, what else?
Mike: What do you mean, "what else?"
 Ken: Well, I always make oil and vinegar, but if you want, we could try something else.
Mike: Does that mean you don't like it when I make other dressings?

   Ken: No, I like it. Go ahead. Make something else.
Mike: Not if you want oil and vinegar.
   Ken: I don't. Make a yogurt dressing.

Mike makes yogurt dressing, tastes it, and makes a face.

   Ken: Isn't it good?
Mike: I don't know how to make yogurt dressing.
   Ken: Well, if you don't like it, throw it out.
Mike: Never mind.
   Ken: What never mind? It's just a little yogurt.
Mike: You're making a big deal about nothing.
   Ken: *You* are!

How could Mike and Ken end up having a fight—and really feeling bad—over salad dressing? They misread each other's frames; each stayed within his own frame; and both interpreted intentions in terms of the overriding frame, "Do you care about me?"

The trouble started when Ken responded to Mike's question by saying, "Oil and vinegar, what else?" Mike heard this—and many others hear it—as a demand for the kind of dressing he likes: oil and vinegar. And the tag question "what else?" seemed to have a metamessage, "You're a jerk for asking. You should have known."

Mike had expected to be given the option "Make whatever you want" or at most a vague preference like "How about something creamy?" In fact, Ken *was* giving Mike the option. But he was doing it by speaking ironically, implying, "Oh, you know me. I'm not very imaginative. I always make the same thing. So don't go by me; make whatever you want."

Ken's "what else?" was framed as ironic self-mockery by his intonation and tone of voice. But Mike missed those signals because it didn't seem natural to him to use irony in that way at such a time. Instead Mike thought he recognized the frame "being demanding and bossy." This didn't surprise him one bit because he often felt Ken was bossing him around. What really hurt was Ken's implication that there was something wrong with him for asking, introducing the frame "put-down" when Mike was being considerate. Mike began to feel sorry for himself for having such a selfish and bossy lover.

Mike and Ken both tried to clear up the misunderstanding, but everything they did to make things better made them worse. When Mike missed his original irony, Ken suggested "make yogurt dressing" as proof of good faith. "Yogurt dressing" stood for "something else." But Mike heard "yogurt dressing" as standing for "yogurt dressing." So he heard Ken first demanding oil and vinegar, then demanding yogurt dressing, then ordering him to throw it out. He saw Ken getting bossier by the minute.

For his part, Ken could not understand why Mike stubbornly refused to make whatever salad dressing he wanted, prepared a dressing he didn't want to make, refused to chuck it when he didn't like the way it turned out—and got huffy when Ken was trying so hard to be agreeable.

As Mike and Ken went about their lives talking in their habitual ways, such style differences kept cropping up. Mike saw more and more evidence that Ken was demanding and selfish and putting him down, and Ken saw more and more evidence that Mike was temperamental and hypersensitive. Mike's feelings were hurt about twenty times a day, and Ken felt he couldn't open his mouth without unintentionally saying the wrong thing. All these misunderstandings—which they did not see as misunderstandings but as the other's personality defects or lack of caring—undermined their sincere love for each other and made daily life together a series of disappointments and hurts. Eventually they split up.

Mike and Ken never really knew how they ended up arguing over yogurt dressing. The feeling of not knowing what one has said to set things off is common—and maddening. The writer Georges Simenon wrote in his diary, "I don't know what I said that sparked a crisis. Words are like drops of acid on a burn." Often, focusing on the words spoken precludes figuring out what sparked a crisis, because the culprits are not words but tone of voice, intonation, and unstated implications and assumptions.

Complementary Schismogenesis

When Mike and Ken quarreled about yogurt dressing, they were really quarreling about love: Do you consider my wishes? Why do you attack me when I am being nice to you? Ironically, as they tried to recoup lost good will, they exhibited more and more exaggerated forms of the behavior that was causing a negative reaction in the other. Ken got bossier, and Mike got more temperamental, in reaction to the other's reaction to their perceived bossiness and hypersensitivity. This process has been called by Gregory Bateson *complementary schismogenesis*: a process by which two people exhibit more and more extreme forms of the behaviors that trigger in the other increasing manifestations of an incongruent behavior, in an ever-worsening spiral.

Mary Catherine Bateson gives this explanation of Gregory Bateson's notion of complementary schismogenesis:

> The situation he depicted is something like the practical joke that can be played using a dual-control electric blanket. If you reverse the controls, the first attempt by either person to make an adjustment will set off a cycle of worsening maladjustment—I am cold, I set the controls beside me higher, you get too hot and turn your controls down, so I get colder, and so on. The attempt to correct actually increases the error. . . . Once the wiring is in the wrong place, efforts at change are palliative or worse.

Differences in conversational style are analogous to having the wiring in the wrong place. For a simple example of com-

plementary schismogenesis in conversation, imagine that one
person is talking slightly louder than the other. If their styles
are similar, one or the other or both might adjust their level
of loudness so they'd end up more or less the same. But if
their ideas about how loud it's normal to speak are different,
each speaker will be made uncomfortable by the other's volume. The slightly louder one might try to encourage the
softer one to speak up by getting a little louder—to set a
good example. And the slightly softer one might try to encourage the louder one to speak more softly by setting a good
example of softer speech. As each tries harder to remedy the
situation, one gets louder and louder while the other gets
softer and softer until one is shouting and the other whispering. Each unintentionally provokes the other to intensify the
offending behavior. As a result, rather than getting more
similar, they get more and more different. That is complementary schismogenesis: creating a split in a mutually aggravating way.

Observing such behavior from the outside, or looking back
on it, we may think it irrational or stubborn to do more of
the same instead of changing tactics. But at the time, we
don't think of changing tactics because ways of talking seem
self-evidently appropriate. We look elsewhere for the causes
of trouble and go on talking in the only way we know to go
about talking.

Miriam was trying to disengage from her friendship with
Liz because she had become aware that the closer she and Liz
got, the more she found herself scared to say anything for
fear of provoking Liz to snap at or confront her. One day Liz
asked directly why Miriam was backing off. Miriam wanted
to be honest but she also had a deep and habitual inclination
not to say anything that would hurt the person she was talking to. So she told Liz that she had been busy and really
wasn't seeing anyone much, which was true as far as it went.
"That's not it!" Liz snapped, accurately. "You can make time
if you want to." Feeling attacked and accused by the

abruptness of Liz's reaction, Miriam floundered around and finally admitted, "I guess maybe I kind of wanted to back off a bit, like maybe we were getting too involved in a way that, you know, maybe was sort of negative." "That's more like it," Liz said, satisfied.

Yet this was one of their last conversations, because it was an instance of the reason Miriam was trying to disengage. The direct, accusatory way Liz snapped, "That's not it!," though accurate, made Miriam feel overpowered, cornered, and criticized. It made her feel bad. In a similar situation, she would have said something like "That may be part of it, but I get the feeling there's something else too, because I know even when I'm busy I can make time to see people if I really want to." In response to something like that, Miriam would have been able to edge her way to the truth. Instead, knowing that Liz was likely to lash out at her and jerk her into admissions she'd rather make gradually had the effect of making Miriam more tentative, roundabout, and evasive in talking to Liz—just the sort of verbal dodging that got on Liz's nerves and made her want to take Miriam by the collar and shake her to the point.

Who's Reacting?

Communication is a system. Everything that is said is simultaneously an instigation and a reaction, a reaction and an instigation. Most of us tend to focus on the first part of that process while ignoring or downplaying the second. We see ourselves as reacting to what others say and do, without realizing that their actions or words are in part reactions to ours, and that our reactions to them won't be the end of the process but rather will trigger more reactions, in a continuous stream. When problems arise, we sincerely try to solve them, but we're thinking of intentions, not style. So when styles differ, trying harder to make things better often means doing more of the same—and making things worse.

The Paradox of Love and Marriage

Why is it so common to find stylistic differences among partners in close relationships? I suspect it is a paradox built into
our system of self-arranged marriage. We often choose our
partners on the basis of romantic attraction, which is sparked
by cultural difference. But as we settle in for the long haul,
we expect friendly companionship. And that is most often
found in cultural similarity. So the seeds of disappointment
are sown in the same field as those of love.

Yet persistent struggles of the sort described are common
among partners from the same country, the same town—
even the same block. This is because many of our closest and
most precious relationships are between men and women,
and men and women are guaranteed to have differences in
style. Male-female conversation is always cross-cultural. The
next chapter shows why and how.

CHAPTER EIGHT

Talk in the Intimate Relationship: His and Hers

Male-female conversation is cross-cultural communication. Culture is simply a network of habits and patterns gleaned from past experience, and women and men have different past experiences. From the time they're born, they're treated differently, talked to differently, and talk differently as a result. Boys and girls grow up in different worlds, even if they grow up in the same house. And as adults they travel in different worlds, reinforcing patterns established in childhood. These cultural differences include differing expectations about the role of talk in relationships and how it fulfills that role.

Chapter Seven showed how complementary schismogenesis—a mutually aggravating spiral—can intensify style differences in ongoing relationships. To see how male-female differences in conversational style can cause misunderstandings that lead to complementary schismogenesis in close relationships, let's start by seeing what some of those differences are.

He Said/She Said: His and Her
Conversational Styles

Everyone knows that as a relationship becomes long-term, its terms change. But women and men often differ in how they expect them to change. Many women feel, "After all this time, you should know what I want without my telling you." Many men feel, "After all this time, we should be able to tell each other what we want."

These incongruent expectations capture one of the key differences between men and women. As explained in Chapter Two, communication is always a matter of balancing conflicting needs for involvement and independence. Though everyone has both these needs, women often have a relatively greater need for involvement, and men a relatively greater need for independence. Being understood without saying what you mean gives a payoff in involvement, and that is why women value it so highly.

If you want to be understood without saying what you mean explicitly in words, you must convey meaning somewhere else—in how words are spoken, or by metamessages. Thus it stands to reason that women are often more attuned than men to the metamessages of talk. When women surmise meaning in this way, it seems mysterious to men, who call it "women's intuition" (if they think it's right) or "reading things in" (if they think it's wrong). Indeed, it could be wrong, since metamessages are not on record. And even if it is right, there is still the question of scale: How significant are the metamessages that are there?

Chapter Two also explained that metamessages are a form of indirectness. Women are more likely to be indirect, and to try to reach agreement by negotiation. Another way to understand this preference is that negotiation allows a display of solidarity, which women prefer to the display of power (even though, as Chapter Six shows, the aim may be the same—getting what you want). Unfortunately, power and solidarity are bought with the same currency: Ways of talking intended to create solidarity have the simultaneous effect of framing power differences. When they think they're being nice, women often end up appearing deferential and unsure of themselves or of what they want.

When styles differ, misunderstandings are always rife. As their differing styles create misunderstandings, women and men try to clear them up by talking things out. These pitfalls are compounded in talks between men and women because they have different ways of going about talking things out, and different assumptions about the significance of going about it.

The rest of this chapter illustrates these differences, explains their origins in children's patterns of play, and shows the effects when women and men talk to each other in the context of intimate relationships in our culture.

Women Listen for Metamessages

Sylvia and Harry celebrated their fiftieth wedding anniversary at a mountain resort. Some of the guests were at the resort for the whole weekend, others just for the evening of the celebration: a cocktail party followed by a sitdown dinner. The manager of the dining room approached Sylvia during dinner. "Since there's so much food tonight," he said, "and the hotel prepared a fancy dessert, and everyone already ate at the cocktail party anyway, how about cutting and serving the anniversary cake at lunch tomorrow?" Sylvia asked the advice of the others at her table. All the men agreed: "Sure, that makes sense. Save the cake for tomorrow." All the women disagreed: "No, the party is tonight. Serve the cake tonight." The men were focusing on the message: the cake as food. The women were thinking of the met-amessage: Serving a special cake frames an occasion as a celebration.

Why are women more attuned to metamessages? Because they are more focused on involvement, that is, on relationships among people, and it is through metamessages that relationships among people are established and maintained. If you want to take the temperature and check the vital signs of a relationship, the barometers to check are its meta-messages: what is said and how.

Everyone can see these signals, but whether or not we pay attention to them is another matter—a matter of being sensitized. Once you are sensitized, you can't roll your antennae back in; they're stuck in the extended position.

When interpreting meaning, it is possible to pick up signals that weren't intentionally sent out, like an innocent flock of birds on a radar screen. The birds are there—and the signals women pick up are there—but they may not mean what the interpreter thinks they mean. For example, Maryellen looks at Larry and asks, "What's wrong?" because his brow is furrowed. Since he was only thinking about lunch, her expression of concern makes him feel under scrutiny.

The difference in focus on messages and metamessages can give men and women different points of view on almost any comment. Harriet complains to Morton, "Why don't you ask me how my day was?" He replies, "If you have something to tell me, tell me. Why do you have to be invited?" The reason is that she wants the metamessage of interest: evidence that he cares how her day was, regardless of whether or not she has something to tell.

A lot of trouble is caused between women and men by, of all things, pronouns. Women often feel hurt when their partners use "I" or "me" in a situation in which they would use "we" or "us." When Morton announces, "I think I'll go for a walk," Harriet feels specifically uninvited, though Morton later claims she would have been welcome to join him. She felt locked out by his use of "I" and his omission of an invitation: "Would you like to come?" Metamessages can be seen in what is not said as well as what is said.

It's difficult to straighten out such misunderstandings because each one feels convinced of the logic of his or her position and the illogic—or irresponsibility—of the other's. Harriet knows that she always asks Morton how his day was, and that she'd never announce, "I'm going for a walk," without inviting him to join her. If he talks differently to her, it must be that he feels differently. But Morton wouldn't feel unloved if Harriet didn't ask about his day, and he would feel free to ask, "Can I come along?," if she announced she was taking a walk. So he can't believe she is justified in feeling responses he knows he wouldn't have.

Messages and Metamessages in Talk Between . . . Grown Ups?

These processes are dramatized with chilling yet absurdly amusing authenticity in Jules Feiffer's play *Grown Ups*. To get a closer look at what happens when men and women focus on different levels of talk in talking things out, let's look at what happens in this play.

Jake criticizes Louise for not responding when their daughter, Edie, called her. His comment leads to a fight, even though they're both aware that this one incident is not in itself important.

> Jake: Look, I don't care if it's important or not, when a kid calls its mother the mother should answer.
> Louise: Now I'm a bad mother.
> Jake: I didn't say that.
> Louise: It's in your stare.
> Jake: Is that another thing you know? My stare?

Louise ignores Jake's message—the question of whether or not she responded when Edie called—and goes for the meta-message: his implication that she's a bad mother, which Jake insistently disclaims. When Louise explains the signals she's reacting to, Jake not only discounts them but is angered at being held accountable not for what he said but for how he looked—his stare.

As the play goes on, Jake and Louise replay and intensify these patterns:

> Louise: If I'm such a terrible mother, do you want a divorce?
>
> Jake: I do not think you're a terrible mother and no, thank you, I do not want a divorce. Why is it that whenever I bring up any difference between us you ask me if I want a divorce?

The more he denies any meaning beyond the message, the more she blows it up, the more adamantly he denies it, and so on:

> Jake: I have brought up one thing that you do with Edie that I don't think you notice that I have noticed for some time but which I have deliberately not brought up before because I had hoped you would notice it for yourself and stop doing it and also—frankly, baby, I have to say this—I knew if I brought it up we'd get into exactly the kind of circular argument we're in right now. And I wanted to avoid it. But I haven't and we're in it, so now, with your permission, I'd like to talk about it.
>
> Louise: You don't see how that puts me down?
>
> Jake: What?
>
> Louise: If you think I'm so stupid why do you go on living with me?
>
> Jake: *Dammit! Why can't anything ever be simple around here?!*

It can't be simple because Louise and Jake are responding to different levels of communication. As in Bateson's example of the dual-control electric blanket with crossed wires, each one intensifies the energy going to a different aspect of the problem. Jake tries to clarify his point by overelaborating it, which gives Louise further evidence that he's condescending to her, making it even less likely that she will address his point rather than his condescension.

What pushes Jake and Louise beyond anger to rage is their different perspectives on metamessages. His refusal to admit that his statements have implications and overtones denies her authority over her own feelings. Her attempts to interpret what he didn't say and put the metamessage into the message makes him feel she's putting words into his mouth—denying his authority over his own meaning.

The same thing happens when Louise tells Jake that he is being manipulated by Edie:

Louise: Why don't you ever make her come to see you? Why do you always go to her?

Jake: You want me to play power games with a nine year old? I want her to know I'm interested in her. Someone around here has to show interest in her.

Louise: You love her more than I do.

Jake: I didn't say that.

Louise: Yes, you did.

Jake: You don't know how to listen. You have never learned how to listen. It's as if listening to you is a foreign language.

Again, Louise responds to his implication—this time, that he loves Edie more because he runs when she calls. And yet again, Jake cries literal meaning, denying he meant any more than he said.

Throughout their argument, the point to Louise is her feelings—that Jake makes her feel put down—but to him the

point is her actions—that she doesn't always respond when
Edie calls:

> Louise: You talk about what I do to Edie, what do you
>   think you do to me?
> Jake: This is not the time to go into what we do to each
>   other.

Since she will talk only about the metamessage, and he will
talk only about the message, neither can get satisfaction from
their talk, and they end up where they started—only an-
grier:

> Jake: That's not the point!
> Louise: It's *my* point.
> Jake: It's hopeless!
> Louise: Then get a divorce.

American conventional wisdom (and many of our parents
and English teachers) tell us that meaning is conveyed by
words, so men who tend to be literal about words are supported by conventional wisdom. They may not simply deny
but actually miss the cues that are sent by how words are
spoken. If they sense something about it, they may nonetheless discount what they sense. After all, it wasn't said. Sometimes that's a dodge—a plausible defense rather than a gut
feeling. But sometimes it is a sincere conviction. Women are
also likely to doubt the reality of what they sense. If they
don't doubt it in their guts, they nonetheless may lack the
arguments to support their position and thus are reduced to
repeating, "You said it. You did so." Knowing that metamessages are a real and fundamental part of communication
makes it easier to understand and justify what they feel.

"Talk to Me"

An article in a popular newspaper reports that one of the five most common complaints of wives about their husbands is "He doesn't listen to me anymore." Another is "He doesn't talk to me anymore." Political scientist Andrew Hacker noted that lack of communication, while high on women's lists of reasons for divorce, is much less often mentioned by men. Since couples are parties to the same conversations, why are women more dissatisfied with them than men? Because what they expect is different, as well as what they see as the significance of talk itself.

First, let's consider the complaint "He doesn't talk to me."

The Strong Silent Type

One of the most common stereotypes of American men is the strong silent type. Jack Kroll, writing about Henry Fonda on the occasion of his death, used the phrases "quiet power," "abashed silences," "combustible catatonia," and "sense of power held in check." He explained that Fonda's goal was not to let anyone see "the wheels go around," not to let the "machinery" show. According to Kroll, the resulting silence was effective on stage but devastating to Fonda's family.

The image of a silent father is common and is often the model for the lover or husband. But what attracts us can become flypaper to which we are unhappily stuck. Many women find the strong silent type to be a lure as a lover but a lug as a husband. Nancy Schoenberger begins a poem with the lines "It was your silence that hooked me,/ so like my father's." Adrienne Rich refers in a poem to the "husband who is frustratingly mute." Despite the initial attraction of such quintessentially male silence, it may begin to feel, to a woman in a long-term relationship, like a brick wall against which she is banging her head.

In addition to these images of male and female behavior—both the result and the cause of them—are differences in how women and men view the role of talk in relationships as well as how talk accomplishes its purpose. These differences have their roots in the settings in which men and women learn to have conversations: among their peers, growing up.

Growing Up Male and Female

Children whose parents have foreign accents don't speak with accents. They learn to talk like their peers. Little girls and little boys learn how to have conversations as they learn how to pronounce words: from their playmates. Between the ages of five and fifteen, when children are learning to have conversations, they play mostly with friends of their own sex. So it's not surprising that they learn different ways of having and using conversations.

Anthropologists Daniel Maltz and Ruth Borker point out that boys and girls socialize differently. Little girls tend to play in small groups or, even more common, in pairs. Their social life usually centers around a best friend, and friendships are made, maintained, and broken by talk—especially "secrets." If a little girl tells her friend's secret to another little girl, she may find herself with a new best friend. The secrets themselves may or may not be important, but the fact of telling them is all-important. It's hard for newcomers to get into these tight groups, but anyone who is admitted is treated as an equal. Girls like to play cooperatively; if they can't cooperate, the group breaks up.

Little boys tend to play in larger groups, often outdoors, and they spend more time doing things than talking. It's easy for boys to get into the group, but not everyone is accepted as an equal. Once in the group, boys must jockey for their status in it. One of the most important ways they do this is through talk: verbal display such as telling stories and jokes, challenging and sidetracking the verbal displays of other boys, and withstanding other boys' challenges in order to maintain their own story—and status. Their talk is often competitive talk about who is best at what.

From Children to Grown Ups

Feiffer's play is ironically named *Grown Ups* because adult men and women struggling to communicate often sound like children: "You said so!" "I did not!" The reason is that when they grow up, women and men keep the divergent attitudes and habits they learned as children—which they don't recognize as attitudes and habits but simply take for granted as ways of talking.

Women want their partners to be a new and improved version of a best friend. This gives them a soft spot for men who tell them secrets. As Jack Nicholson once advised a guy in a movie: "Tell her about your troubled childhood—that always gets 'em." Men expect to *do* things together and don't feel anything is missing if they don't have heart-to-heart talks all the time.

If they do have heart-to-heart talks, the meaning of those talks may be opposite for men and women. To many women, the relationship is working as long as they can talk things out. To many men, the relationship isn't working out if they have to keep working it over. If she keeps trying to get talks going to save the relationship, and he keeps trying to avoid them because he sees them as weakening it, then each one's efforts to preserve the relationship appear to the other as reckless endangerment.

How to Talk Things Out

If talks (of any kind) do get going, men's and women's ideas about how to conduct them may be very different. For example, Dora is feeling comfortable and close to Tom. She settles into a chair after dinner and begins to tell him about a problem at work. She expects him to ask questions to show he's interested; reassure her that he understands and that what she feels is normal; and return the intimacy by telling her a problem of his. Instead, Tom sidetracks her story, cracks jokes about it, questions her interpretation of the problem, and gives her advice about how to solve it and avoid such problems in the future.

All of these responses, natural to men, are unexpected to women, who interpret them in terms of their own habits—negatively. When Tom comments on side issues or cracks jokes, Dora thinks he doesn't care about what she's saying and isn't really listening. If he challenges her reading of what went on, she feels he is criticizing her and telling her she's crazy, when what she wants is to be reassured that she's not. If he tells her how to solve the problem, it makes her feel as if she's the patient to his doctor—a metamessage of condescension, echoing male one-upmanship compared to the female etiquette of equality. Because he doesn't volunteer information about his problems, she feels he's implying .he doesn't have any.

Complementary schismogenesis can easily set in: His way of responding to her bid for intimacy makes her feel distant from him. She tries harder to regain intimacy the only way she knows how—by revealing more and more about herself. He tries harder by giving more insistent advice. The more problems she exposes, the more incompetent she feels, until they both see her as emotionally draining and problem-ridden. When his efforts to help aren't appreciated, he wonders why she asks for his advice if she doesn't want to take it.

"You're Not Listening to Me"

The other complaint wives make about their husbands is "He doesn't listen to me anymore." The wives may be right that their husbands aren't listening, if they don't value the telling of problems and secrets to establish rapport. But some of the time men feel unjustly accused: "I *was* listening." And some of the time, they're right. They were.

Whether or not someone is listening only that person can really know. But we judge whether or not we think others are listening by signals we can see—not only their verbal responses but also their eye contact and little listening noises like "mhm," "uh-huh," and "yeah." These listening noises give the go-ahead for talk; if they are misplaced along the track, they can quickly derail a chugging conversation.

Maltz and Borker also report that women and men have different ways of showing that they're listening. In the listening role, women make—and expect—more of these noises. So when men are listening to women, they are likely to make too few such noises for the women to feel the men are really listening. And when women are listening to men, making more such listening noises than men expect may give the impression they're impatient or exaggerating their show of interest.

Even worse, what women and men mean by such noises may be different. Does "uh-huh" or "mhm" mean you agree with what you heard, or just that you heard and you're following? Maltz and Borker contend that women tend to use these noises just to show they're listening and understanding. Men tend to use them to show they agree. So one reason women make more listening noises may be that women are listening more than men are agreeing with what they hear.

In addition to problems caused by differences in how many signals are given, there is bound to be trouble as a result of the difference in how they're used. If a woman cheers a man on in his talk by saying "mhm" and "yeah" and "uh-huh" all over the place, and it later comes out that she disagrees with what he said, he may feel she misled him (thereby reinforcing his stereotype of women as unreliable). Conversely, if a man sits through a woman's talk and follows all she says but doesn't agree, he's not going to shower her with "uh-huh's"—and she's going to think he's not paying attention.

Notice that the difference in how women and men use listening noises is in keeping with their focus in communication. Using the noises to show "I'm listening; go on" serves the relationship level of talk. Using them to show what one thinks of what is being said is a response to the content of talk. So men and women are being stylistically consistent in their interactive inconsistency.

"Why Don't You Talk About Something Interesting?"

Sometimes when men and women feel the other isn't paying attention, they're right. And this may be because their assumptions about what's interesting are different. Muriel gets bored when Daniel goes on and on about the stock market or the world soccer match. He gets bored when she goes on and on about details of her daily life or the lives of people he doesn't even know.

It seems natural to women to tell and hear about what happened today, who turned up at the bus stop, who called and what she said, not because these details are important in themselves but because the telling of them proves involvement—that you care about each other, that you have a best friend. Knowing you will be able to tell these things later makes you feel less alone as you go along the lone path of a day. And if you don't tell, you are sending a metamessage about the relationship—curtailing it, clipping its wings.

Since it is not natural to men to use talk in this way, they focus on the inherent insignificance of the details. What they find worth telling are facts about such topics as sports, politics, history, or how things work. Women often perceive the telling of facts as lecturing, which not only does not carry (for them) a metamessage of rapport, but carries instead a metamessage of condescension: I'm the teacher, you're the student. I'm knowledgeable, you're ignorant.

A *New Yorker* cartoon shows a scene—probably the source of a thousand cartoons (and a million conversations)—of a breakfast table, with a husband reading a newspaper while the wife is trying to talk to him. The husband says, "You want to talk? Get a newspaper. We'll talk about what's in the newspaper." It's funny because everyone knows that what's in the newspaper is not what the wife wants to talk about.

Conversations About Conversations

When women talk about what seems obviously interesting to them, their conversations often include reports of conversations. Tone of voice, timing, intonation, and wording are all re-created in the telling in order to explain—dramatize, really—the experience that is being reported. If men tell about an incident and give a brief summary instead of re-creating what was said and how, the women often feel that the essence of the experience is being omitted. If the woman asks, "What exactly did he say?," and "How did he say it?," the man probably can't remember. If she continues to press him, he may feel as if he's being grilled.

All these different habits have repercussions when the man and the woman are talking about their relationship. He feels out of his element, even one down. She claims to recall exactly what he said, and what she said, and in what sequence, and she wants him to account for what he said. He can hardly account for it since he has forgotten exactly what was said—if not the whole conversation. She secretly suspects he's only pretending not to remember, and he secretly suspects that she's making up the details.

One woman reported such a problem as being a matter of her boyfriend's poor memory. It is unlikely, however, that his problem was poor memory in general. The question is what types of material each person remembers or forgets.

Frances was sitting at her kitchen table talking to Edward, when the toaster did something funny. Edward began to explain why it did it. Frances tried to pay attention, but very early in his explanation, she realized she was completely lost. She felt very stupid. And indications were that he thought so too.

Later that day they were taking a walk. He was telling her about a difficult situation in his office that involved a complex network of interrelationships among a large number of people. Suddenly he stopped and said, "I'm sure you can't keep track of all these people." "Of course I can," she said, and she retraced his story with all the characters in place, all the details right. He was genuinely impressed. She felt very smart.

How could Frances be both smart and stupid? Did she have a good memory or a bad one? Frances's and Edward's abilities to follow, remember, and recount depended on the subject—and paralleled her parents' abilities to follow and remember. Whenever Frances told her parents about people in her life, her mother could follow with no problem, but her father got lost as soon as she introduced a second character. "Now who was that?" he'd ask. "Your boss?" "No, my boss is Susan. This was my friend." Often he'd still be in the previous story. But whenever she told them about her work, it was her mother who would get lost as soon as she mentioned a second step: "That was your tech report?" "No, I handed my tech report in last month. This was a special project."

Frances's mother and father, like many other men and women, had honed their listening and remembering skills in different arenas. Their experience talking to other men and other women gave them practice in following different kinds of talk.

Knowing whether and how we are likely to report events later influences whether and how we pay attention when they happen. As women listen to and take part in conversations, knowing they may talk about them later makes them more likely to pay attention to exactly what is said and how. Since most men aren't in the habit of making such reports, they are less likely to pay much attention at the time. On the other hand, many women aren't in the habit of paying attention to scientific explanations and facts because they don't expect to have to perform in public by reciting them—just as those who aren't in the habit of entertaining others by telling jokes "can't" remember jokes they've heard, even though they listened carefully enough to enjoy them.

So women's conversations with their women friends keep them in training for talking about their relationships with men, but many men come to such conversations with no training at all—and an uncomfortable sense that this really isn't their event.

"What Do You Mean, My Dear?"

Most of us place enormous emphasis on the importance of a primary relationship. We regard the ability to maintain such relationships as a sign of mental health—our contemporary metaphor for being a good person.

Yet our expectations of such relationships are nearly— maybe in fact—impossible. When primary relationships are between women and men, male-female differences contribute to the impossibility. We expect partners to be both romantic interests and best friends. Though women and men may have fairly similar expectations for romantic interests, obscuring their differences when relationships begin, they have very different ideas about how to be friends, and these are the differences that mount over time.

In conversations between friends who are not lovers, small misunderstandings can be passed over or diffused by breaks in contact. But in the context of a primary relationship, differences can't be ignored, and the pressure cooker of continued contact keeps both people stewing in the juice of accumulated minor misunderstandings. And stylistic differences are sure to cause misunderstandings—not, ironically, in matters such as sharing values and interests or understanding each other's philosophies of life. These large and significant yet palpable issues can be talked about and agreed on. It is far harder to achieve congruence—and much more surprising and troubling that it is hard—in the simple day-to-day matters of the automatic rhythms and nuances of talk. Nothing in our backgrounds or in the media (the present-day counterpart to religion or grandparents' teachings) prepares us for this failure. If two people share so much in terms of point of view and basic values, how can they continually get into fights about insignificant matters?

If you find yourself in such a situation and you don't know about differences in conversational style, you assume something's wrong with your partner or you, or you for having chosen your partner. At best, if you are forward thinking and generous minded, you may absolve individuals and blame the relationship. But if you know about differences in conversational style, you can accept that there are differences in habits and assumptions about how to have conversation, show interest, be considerate, and so on. You may not always correctly interpret your partner's intentions, but you will know that if you get a negative impression, it may not be what was intended—and neither are your responses unfounded. If he says he really is interested even though he doesn't seem to be, maybe you should believe what he says and not what you sense.

Sometimes explaining assumptions can help. If a man starts to tell a woman what to do to solve her problem, she may say, "Thanks for the advice but I really don't want to be told what to do. I just want you to listen and say you understand." A man might want to explain, "If I challenge you, it's not to prove you wrong; it's just my way of paying attention to what you're telling me." Both may try either or both to modify their ways of talking and to try to accept what the other does. The important thing is to know that what seem like bad intentions may really be good intentions expressed in a different conversational style. We have to give up our conviction that, as Robin Lakoff put it, "Love means never having to say 'What do you mean?.'"

CHAPTER NINE

The Intimate Critic

The commonest social encounters are fraught with a thousand possible failures, not the least of which is the failure of nerve. That's one of the reasons many people prefer to appear in public as partners: to have an ally in the social fray, to present to the world the solid flank that sometimes offends those who appear as single people—like trapeze artists performing without a net. As members of couples, many feel that if they blunder it will matter less because their ally will think they're terrific no matter what.

But here's the trick of fate: As often as not, the intimate ally becomes an intimate critic. Not only does your partner not see you as charming despite your social lapses, but worse, your partner sees lapses when no one else sees them or, worst of all, sees lapses when you have committed no error at all, but have simply done or said something in a way that is peculiarly and recognizably your own.

By a strange alchemy, the quirks and manners that annoy the intimate critic are the very same elements of personal style that seemed irresistibly charming in the beginning.

Small indiscretions, minor false notes that would pass unnoticed or be forgotten had you been at the party alone are highlighted, spotlighted, emblazoned in memory by extended analysis in the car on the way home, and enlarged by association with past failings.

Every social encounter is rich with blunders, inanities, and foolishness. Very little of what is said is really apt, still less important, still less eloquent. But people accept, respond to, echo, laugh with, and generally appreciate the stumbling attempts others make at conversation because they appreciate the show of interest, the willingness to take part. Only of ourselves are we hypercritical: Why did I say that? How dumb of me. Only of ourselves—and of the people closest to us.

We don't openly criticize ourselves, or if we do, the effect is charming: another show of eagerness to please. But if we openly criticize someone else, the effect is anything but charming. Witnessing someone being shown up as a social incompetent makes onlookers as uncomfortable as the criticized party.

The Means of Criticism: Help We Can Do Without

Intimate criticism is epidemic wherever people are close: in families, between lovers, among traveling companions. Marilyn and Gerald were visiting France. One evening, as they were talking with French friends, Marilyn carefully planned a sentence in what she could recall of her high-school French. When there was a pause in the conversation, she began, "*Alors* . . ." A French neighbor turned to her and asked, "*Alors, quoi?*" Delighted to have succeeded thus far, she was about to continue, when Gerald burst in, explaining to the others (in his better-than-hers but still halting French) her habit of filling in conversational pauses. He thought she had talked herself onto a linguistic limb: that she'd misused *"Alors"* and had nothing more to say. She was angry not because he had cut her off but because he had made her look incompetent. His familiarity with her style made him see weakness where she had felt strength, and his attempt to help her out communicated his vision of her weakness to the others. Generally, the best help one can give to those one thinks have done or said something wrong is to pretend they haven't.

Trying to help out is one way (a subtle one) of being critical. There are many others.

Sarcasm

A common means of criticism—in public or in private—is sarcasm. For example, Timothy met his ex-wife at their children's school during an international fair featuring food from various countries. He approached her with a friendly greeting. She asked if he had bought anything to eat; he told her he had bought a croissant. She said with a smirk, "Adventurous, huh?" Zap. By describing his behavior in a way that obviously did not apply, she was letting him know that she thought he should be more adventurous, reducing his French croissant to a dull piece of bread.

Timothy's reaction to his ex-wife's remark was intensified by their history. She'd often made him feel bad about being too cautious, too conservative. In an ongoing relationship, each current criticism packs the punches of all the others that have gone before. That's part of the reason long-time partners and family members often explode in response to minor offenses.

Timothy's dismay was aggravated by the frame shift introduced by his ex-wife's sarcasm. Since he had been operating in a friendly frame, the stab of her criticism was deepened by its unexpectedness. His defenses were down, and he was hurt to see that his good will was not matched by hers.

A frame change is also involved in the pain of being criticized for something that had previously been a source of satisfaction. Ted is a life-of-the-party type. But when he was pleased and proud that he'd kept the party rolling with his stories and jokes, his wife told him afterward that he'd made a fool of himself and neglected her. Wham! What he had felt to be a success was reframed as a failure.

Criticism in Praise

One of the most subtle ways of criticizing the person you're talking to is praising someone else. Turkish has an expression to correct for this if it's not so intended. A Turk who praises one person while speaking to another can say *"Sizden iyi olmasin,"* which means "May she (he) not be better than you"—in other words, "Don't think (as you might) that my praising someone else means I think you are unworthy of similar praise."

Some parents use the tactic of praising another child in order to point out the true path to their own: "Look, Billy. See how neat Tommy keeps his room?" The result, unfortunately, is often not to make Billy keep his room neater but (especially if such lessons are frequent) to make him feel criticized, inadequate, and unloved—and to hate Tommy.

Co-workers also experience such twinges—sometimes warranted, sometimes not. The organizer of an impending conference was at first attentive but finally offended when a colleague raved about how well the previous year's conference had been run—by somebody else. What started out sounding like constructive suggestions began to reek of the metamessage "You'll never do as well as last year's organizer."

This metamessage may or may not have been intended; and whether or not it was consciously intended, the person who spoke may or may not have believed that this year's organizer couldn't match last year's. Any device that can be used for a certain purpose can also be mistaken to be serving that purpose when it's not intended to. Many people feel jealous if their partners praise another man or woman. Valid or not, they feel that such praise means the partner is not only praising but comparing. They hear not only "I think she or he is attractive or clever or charming" but also "I think you're less so."

The Critical Stance

As Angela and Conrad left the concert hall, Conrad began to pick apart the performance. Angela got a sinking feeling in her chest. She heard the metamessage "I'm having a rotten time," and, since the time Conrad was having was with her, "I don't like being with you." The more he criticized the musicians, the more certain she felt that the hostility he was expressing toward the piccolo player was really an expression of how he felt about her.

Indeed, it is sometimes true that kicking the dog is a way of expressing anger inspired by a person you can't honorably kick. Yet some people use criticism aimed outward—at other people not present, at inanimate objects—as a means of establishing solidarity with the people they're with. It's a variation of the solidarity-through-complaining device described in Chapter Three. Unfortunately, those who don't expect this critical stance are offended by it; they feel sure that anyone who is so critical of everyone and everything must also be critical of them.

When Emily and Bennet visited Bennet's parents, his father took them all out to dinner. The food wasn't very good, and Emily saw no reason to pretend it was. Given to hyperbole, she remarked, "This is the worst food I ever ate." Bennet's father was mortally offended. Since he was responsible for the dinner, he felt that her criticism of the food was rude to him. To Emily, feeling "like family" with Bennet's family meant her positive attitude toward them went without saying, and criticizing the food was a way of allying herself with them.

Gregory Bateson pointed out that people often fail to distinguish between the map and the territory: the real thing and the thing that represents it symbolically. If we identify strongly with our home, our clothing, our partners, or the restaurant we chose, then criticism aimed at them feels like criticism of us. Sometimes it is, but sometimes it isn't. It's important to remember that the map is not the territory: Some people freely aim arrows at external objects with which people identify, yet they have no intention of wounding people. Quite the contrary, aiming criticism out can be an expression of solidarity with those thus defined as in: "You and me against the world."

"Say It Right!"

Though sometimes criticism is heard when it's not intended, most relationships include enough unmistakable criticism to warrant concern. Women and men are both susceptible to the disease, and both are carriers. But there are forms of it that are particularly common (though certainly not limited) to women or to men.

The article mentioned in Chapter Eight, about common complaints by spouses, reports that husbands feel their wives nag them. Nagging can be about what wasn't done as well as what was. It may be that women frequently criticize partners in this way because they have greater expectations about what a relationship entails (and it may also be the case that men more often fail to fulfill expectations). Many men, for their part, criticize women for not doing things in what they consider the proper and logical way.

After Jim retires, Bea begins to complain that he spends too much time at his desk, doesn't show enough concern for her health, doesn't take enough interest in the grandchildren, watches the news on television during dinner, and refuses to accompany her shopping. A situation in which Jim does offer his company is one in which she'd as soon do without it: in the kitchen, where he finds fault with the way she does things. She cuts onions on the countertop (not intending to cut clear through, but sometimes she slips), doesn't use the proper implements (for example, she uses the point of a knife to open a jar, thus blunting the knife), allows paper to fall in the sink (she takes it out later, but Jim fears for the health of the garbage disposal, which is deathly allergic to paper). Whereas she gets the Venetian blinds to stay up by jerking the cord until it catches, he pleads repeatedly and in vain for her to examine the mechanism so she can efficiently press it once to engage it. Both Jim and Bea are convinced there's a right and wrong way to behave, but Bea focuses her criticism on how Jim treats people (in particular, her), and he focuses on how she treats objects in their environment.

Language is a system of behavior about which many people have strong beliefs of right and wrong. Many women (and some men) criticize their partners for using incorrect grammar, and many men (and some women) criticize their partners for not using words precisely, though in both cases this may simply mean using expressions as they are commonly used. So Stella criticizes Chuck for using double negatives and the word *ain't*, and Saul criticizes Rose for calling the stove an oven or saying "I feel aggravated" when he thinks she should say "irritated" (thus aggravating her irritation).

Correcting English usage is one means of sidetracking someone's story, a listening device mentioned earlier. In a short story by Charles Dickinson, a woman has waited all day for her husband to come home so she can tell him about her meeting with their son's teacher, a meeting he missed because he had to work late:

> "Mr. Frobel told me about an assignment he'd given the class," Fran said. "They have to draw a map of Russia."
> "You mean the Soviet Union. Nobody calls it Russia anymore."
> "Is that important? May I finish?"

Not only does the husband's remark sidetrack the story and focus on something other than the point, but it does so by criticizing Fran for using a word that most people use in daily conversation.

Feiffer captured this too in his play *Grown Ups*. Ignoring what she means, Jake pounces on Louise for getting expressions slightly wrong: "She lies like a glove" for "lies like a rug"; "snitched" to mean "stole," which he thinks should be "snatched"; "put your ten cents in" instead of "two cents"; "flip to attention," which he says "is simply not English." The net result is that Louise feels that Jake thinks (she suspects correctly) that she's not smart enough for him. It may be true that he thinks so; many people regard the use of what they consider correct English usage as a sign of intelligence— an attitude with no basis in fact. What is a fact is that slightly altering common expressions is as common as the expressions themselves and presents no barrier to comprehension.

The tragedy of all these forms of criticism is that they make one feel unheard or even unloved, and the sense of incompetence they engender can long outlive the arguments or discussions that spawned them.

Do It My Way

In many of the preceding examples, the ways of doing things or speaking can be judged incorrect by some external standard. But often critics—male and female—want their intimates to adhere to standards that are not absolute but simply reflect their own cultural conventions, or even their individual habits and styles. And what seems "illogical" is often an expression of a different rather than a lapsed logic.

Returning from their honeymoon, Barbara and Glen were waiting in line for a charter flight back to the States. Barbara struck up a conversation with the woman in front of her. She mentioned that their flight out had been changed from the charter for which they had bought a ticket to a commercial airline. In answer to the woman's question, Barbara explained, "Our travel agent called us—this is our honeymoon—" The woman interjected a quick and smiling "Congratulations"; Barbara smiled too, said, "Thank you," and was about to continue when Glen reached out, stroked her arm, and corrected, "The fact that we're on our honeymoon has nothing to do with how our flight was changed." "I know," Barbara said, looking down. She felt she'd been caught doing something wrong.

But Barbara's mention of her honeymoon was not incorrect. She was glad to tell it; the woman was glad to hear it; it contributed to the rapport they were striking up. Glen would not have tossed in this information in this way, but then he probably wouldn't have started a conversation with a stranger in the first place. The basis for his criticism amounted to little more than "You're not doing it my way."

Since many couples spend much of their time together in social settings, they are likely to hear each other telling stories and engaging in other types of social talk. Unfortunately, the use of talk for social purposes is an area in which men and women often differ. So they have plenty of opportunities to disapprove of each other. And male-female differences are compounded by all the other style differences in using signals and devices discussed in Chapter Three.

Following what Dorothy thought was a great dinner party, Don storms upstairs in anger, accusing her of having dominated. He says she was loud, didn't listen to others, and didn't give others—in particular him—a chance to talk. "You're a big boy," she tells him. "You can say something if you have something to say." He retorts, "You need a crowbar to get into those conversations." At other times, when she shows interest in a guest by asking a lot of questions, Don complains later that she was interrogating the guest— whether or not the guest showed annoyance.

To Don, asking personal questions is obviously rude; to Dorothy it's obviously friendly. To him, a good conversation is slow-paced; to her it's fast-paced. To her, loud overlapping talk is a sign of enthusiasm. To him, it's a sign of not listening. Knowing what we now know about conversational style, we see that neither Don nor Dorothy is right or wrong. But they don't know that. And Dorothy knows her intentions are good; how can her husband so misjudge them? She feels betrayed because she is being attacked by the person who is supposed to be her closest ally.

Ironically, partners feel entitled, even called upon, to correct each other *because* they are allies. Much intimate criticism comes from the desire to improve our partners and other intimates, both for their own good and because we feel they represent us to the world. Since we all have our own ways of doing things, opportunities to correct each other are ubiquitous.

The Origins of Criticism

A common condition that breeds a particularly virulent strain of intimate criticism is adolescence. Many parents are (perhaps necessarily) critical of their children when they are young, but during adolescence, many children turn on their parents with a critical stare that can be devastating. They cannot stand the way their parents walk, dress, and hold a fork. They find their expressions hopelessly dated or awkwardly too current. Simply appearing in public with a parent becomes an ill-masked torment.

The case of adolescents gives a clue to the sources and uses of criticism. For adolescents (as for us all) criticism is a means of protection against the danger of involvement threatening independence. Adolescents must, above all, separate from their parents. If they see their parents as perfect, they want to cling, and they feel inadequate by comparison. Seeing their parents as inadequate makes it easier to let go and makes them feel more competent.

It's the same with couples. Seeing faults in the other allows each to feel more competent by measuring against the most readily available object of comparison. And it is a protection against closeness becoming overwhelming. But feeling constantly criticized becomes in itself one of the dangers of closeness.

At the end of Anne Tyler's novel *Dinner at the Homesick Restaurant*, an old man, Beck Tull, tells his adult son why he walked out on his wife (and children) years before:

> "She wore me out." . . . "Oh, at the start," Beck said, "she thought I was wonderful. You ought to have seen her face when I walked into a room. . . . When your mother and I were first married, everything was perfect. It seemed

I could do no wrong. Then bit by bit I guess she saw my faults. She saw that I was away from home too much and not enough support to her, didn't get ahead in my work, put on weight, drank too much, talked wrong, ate wrong, dressed wrong, drove a car wrong."

This passage gives a sense of the cumulative effect of mounting criticism—both for serious offenses like not being enough support to her and being away from home, and superficial ones like dressing and eating wrong. Beck Tull married his wife because seeing how wonderful she thought he was made him feel wonderful—the joy of closeness. But once she was up close she could see his weaknesses. Then, seeing himself through her eyes made him feel awful.

One way to look at this is that infatuation blinds us to the other's faults, and closeness allows us to see them clearly. But closeness is blinding in a different way. Intimacy can lead us to see more faults than are really there and make them seem larger than they really are.

A Shot in the Dark

The more indirect the means of criticism, the harder it is to deal with. Stan's father questions him about his investments in a way that makes clear he finds them unwise. And Kate's mother sticks close to her side, offering a running commentary that seems to imply her daughter is doing everything wrong in the house.

Watching Kate cook, her mother remarks, "Oh, you put that much salt in the soup?" Kate understands this to mean "You're putting too much salt in the soup"—one more in a visit-long barrage of criticism. But if Kate protests, her mother's plausible defense is: "I was just asking. Why are you so sensitive?" Questions, like sarcasm, are favorite forms of criticism precisely because they are indirect—like shots from a gun with a silencer. The wounded feels the effect, swift and sure, but the source of the attack is hard to locate.

Challenges to critics are difficult to bring off because the critic and the criticized are concerned with different levels of interaction. The critic's attention focuses on one after another action, not on any overall evaluation of the person. Parents know they love their children despite their efforts to get them to do this or that, or this *and* that, in a better way. But the criticized reacts to the metamessage "You're an incompetent person."

When challenged, critics are likely to disclaim (perhaps sincerely) the intent to criticize: "I was just asking" or "just joking" or otherwise "didn't mean anything." If they admit that a remark was critical, they are likely to defend its validity: "You were doing it wrong" or "I said it because it's true." And this may be valid from the point of view of the critic. But it doesn't take into account the effect on the criticized—especially the cumulative effect.

"Ouch, That Hurts!"

While the critic is concerned with the validity of the complaint—the message—the criticized responds to the metamessage of disapproval. Any criticism implies, "I don't think you're a right sort of person," which seems to say, "I don't like you very much." And when criticism comes in a steady stream, as it often does in ongoing relationships, one's sense of being a right sort of person and of being likable is thoroughly undermined—regardless of whether each individual criticism is valid.

One of the most destructive aspects of intimate criticism is that its effects can be lasting. Josie went through years . life happily, if ignorantly, oblivious of innumerable minor faults or faultless habits—a nervous click she sometimes inserts in pauses; automatically yelling "Ow!" when only slightly hurt; a soft fuzz on her upper lip; a tendency to gulp down her drink when others are sipping. But after living with Andy, who continually informed her that he found these and other habits offensive, she was doomed to see them in this nasty light forever. After she divorced Andy, she kept his negative view of her quirks as part of her settlement, etched on her view of herself and shaded in with a general feeling that she was displeasing to be around.

Hand-me-down Criticism

One of the most subtle but also most common and troubling forms of criticism comes masquerading as an impartial report.

A common hit-and-run tactic is to pose as an innocent messenger: "Jerry said he thinks you shouldn't have shown the letter to Molly." In this way, the messenger communicates criticism while deflecting the resultant anger onto Jerry. Most people duly respond to tales-told criticism by feeling angry at or hurt by the quoted critic. But they shouldn't. They should ask, "Why are you telling me this?" Handing down criticism may be a case in which it is appropriate to vent anger on the messenger, the one who chose to deliver the blow.

Secondhand criticism is in many ways more destructive than hearing the same criticism from its source. Criticism spoken directly carries a metamessage of involvement: caring enough to tell. It invites an explanation or self-justification, and the ensuing confrontation is likely to end with a display of renewed solidarity and good will. In contrast, any criticism heard secondhand sounds worse than it would face to face. Words spoken out of our presence strike us as more powerful, just as people we know only by reputation seem larger than life. It is as if by virtue of being overheard, a message is guaranteed to be the truth—what others *really* feel but would not say to us.

This impression is misleading. The truth as it emerges in

one situation is not the real truth but an aspect of the truth
reflected in that situation. Lifting it out and serving it up in
another situation distorts it. What is spoken to a particular
audience is more often than not specially designed for their
consumption. Indeed, it may even have been elicited by
them. We unintentionally turn conversations this way or that
by our own remarks, which constrain the responses we get.

When someone criticizes one person to another, the intention may be to let off steam without hurting anyone. But
if the criticism is reported to the person it was about, it becomes more destructive rather than less. Because it is not
expressed directly, the complaint and the bitterness in response both live on, not tackled, not confronted, not de-
bunked or deskunked by discussion.

For example, an up-and-coming young scholar gave a paper at a meeting of his professional society. He was pleased
to see that one of the leaders in the field—someone whose
work he had read and admired—was in the audience. And
he began to feel elated when his old professor told him that
this star had come to hear his talk because she had heard
about his work. But his pleasure quickly turned to chagrin
when the professor went on to say that the star had reported
being disappointed in what she'd heard.

This chagrin would have congealed into a lasting feeling of
discomfort associated with the senior colleague, if the young
professor had not later found and seized the opportunity to
question her directly. She said, "But didn't he tell you that I
also said you can't expect anyone to say anything in a twelve-
minute talk?" This qualification of the criticism may have
really been uttered in the original comment, or may have
been devised on the spot to soften the blow, but in either
case it defused the criticism and paved the way for a constructive collegial relationship. When one does not have or
take the chance to confront the source of criticism, a sense of
bitterness toward a colleague, friend, or acquaintance can
persist forever, souring an ongoing relationship or impeding
the establishment of a new one.

If repeated criticism can be an irritant in professional or friendly relationships, it can be a poison in families.

Vicki received a letter from her mother expressing distress that Vicki had decided not to spend Christmas with the family. Vicki wrote back explaining her reasons and considered the matter settled. But then she got a call from her sister Jill—a solicitous call, sincerely intended to support Vicki. In the course of showing support, Jill reported that their mother had called her to discuss the problem of Vicki. Jill also reported how she had defended her sister. She'd said, "But, Mama, I didn't come home on my last vacation either." Then she quoted their mother's response: "But that's different. You're in college."

In repeating their mother's conversation to her sister, Jill's intended message was "Mother has judged you unfairly, but I stood up for you." But this well-intentioned message was overshadowed for Vicki by a pack of painful metamessages. First of all, it got across to Vicki that what she thought was settled really wasn't; instead, her mother was still so upset that she had to call someone to talk. (Knowing that Jill was likely to call her sister, Mother might even have used Jill to get this metamessage to Vicki.) Second, Vicki was hurt by the negative comparison with her sister, and angered by the illogic of that comparison: If Jill is still in college, she should be more, not less, obligated to go home for Christmas. Moreover, the image of her mother calling her sister to talk about her suggested a frame: "Family members conferring about the family problem—you!"

Vicki took her mother's reported remarks as the real truth—as did Jill. And when Jill repeated them, she was, after all, accurately repeating what she'd heard. Yet it was she who inadvertently hurt Vicki by repeating a version of the truth that had been specially sculpted for another situation—a conversation with Jill.

The puzzle of Mother's illogic can be solved by putting the remark back where it came from. Jill provoked the comparison when she invoked herself as a counterexample. This forced her mother either to say "You're just as bad" or to come up with some reason—however illogical—to exclude Jill from her criticism.

Siblings, like members of any close-knit group, are prone to this strain of criticism because their relationship to each other is a paradigm of competition for approval, going as far back as Cain and Abel. And the intimacy of family bonds makes it particularly likely that information will be repeated, since exchanging personal information is a means of maintaining intimacy.

A similar case occurred with another pair of sisters, Lynn and Alexandra. At one point in their lives, Lynn was dating a man ten years older than she, and Alexandra was dating a man ten years younger. Long after she stopped dating this man, Lynn harbored a sense of hurt and resentment toward her mother because Alexandra had told her that their mother disapproved more of Lynn's situation than of hers.

Examining Alexandra's conversation with their mother, it is easy to see how the mother came to make such a comparison. Hearing her mother express concern about Lynn, Alexandra protected her sister by putting herself in the line of fire: "But Mom, Tony is ten years younger than I am! What difference does age make?" Suddenly having to include or exempt the daughter she is talking to, Mom chooses to exempt her: "But that's different. You don't have to worry that he will die first and you'll be left alone." There is no reason, in this context, for Mom to mention her concerns about marrying a man ten years younger. It's not that Mom lied to Alexandra or that Alexandra lied to Lynn, but that wrenching an aspect of the truth from one context and hauling it to another alters its effect and is likely to misrepresent the intentions of the original speaker.

Hiding Behind the Curtain

Hearing someone repeat something said about you in your absence puts you in the position, for a fleeting moment, of an eavesdropper on a conversation you weren't supposed to hear, with the added complication that what you hear is necessarily incomplete, out of context, and subject to the alterations that are inevitable when information is filtered through the human imagination.

The tragic events of the novel *Wuthering Heights* were spurred by an incompletely overheard conversation. Heathcliff fled Wuthering Heights—destroying thereby both his life and Cathy's—after overhearing Cathy say to her maid, "It would degrade me to marry Heathcliff now." He did not stay to hear her say, "So he shall never know how I love him," and "He's more myself than I am," and "Every Linton on the face of the earth might melt into nothing, before I could consent to forsake Heathcliff." Heathcliff heard only a part of the conversation, and the overhearing made it seem so much the real truth that he waited to hear no more.

In E. M. Forster's *A Passage to India*, havoc was wreaked by the repeating of an overheard conversation. Dr. Aziz had no intention of carrying through on his *pro forma* invitation to take two English ladies to the Marabar Caves. But an Indian servant overheard one of the ladies say to the other that Indians seem rather forgetful. This remark was repeated and heard, heard and repeated, passed from ear to ear like a whispered sentence in the party game telephone, until it reached Aziz that the women were mortally offended by his omission. He then felt compelled to arrange the trip to the caves that nobody wanted to make, which ended in the novel's disastrous denouement.

The image of others talking about us is always jarring—a

glimpse of a world in which we are not principals but merely the subject of conversation. For a moment it is as if we do not exist, or exist in a drastically reduced form. The rush of pleasure on hearing we have been praised behind our backs is partly a rush of relief—a release of the tension caused by the shock of learning that others have been talking about us at all.

Barred Holds

Understanding the ways and means of intimate criticism that have been discussed in this chapter can be harnessed to provide guidelines for future use—advice both to critics and to the criticized.

Incurable critics (who may be the same people as the criticized, only a moment later) can bear in mind that some forms of criticism are more destructive than others. We all have the power to hurt other people by repeating to them what was said about them in our presence, not theirs. There is probably not one of our acquaintances who has never spoken of us in a way we would not like if we overheard it. It is noble to hold such power in check by not repeating anything except obvious praise, unless careful consideration indicates that it is information a person needs, even though hearing it may hurt. This includes criticism we are disagreeing with or ridiculing, such as "I don't care what anyone says—I don't think you're dumb."

Repeating someone else's critical opinion to bolster our own is effective, but it's a verbal equivalent of brass knuckles: unfair apparatus to enhance the power to wound. Critics who play fair will avoid double whammies like "I think you were wrong and Morris thinks so too." Particularly unfair is reporting criticism while hiding its source— "Someone said this but I can't tell you who"—because it makes the recipient regard all likely and many unlikely sources with suspicion.

Perhaps the unkindest cut of all is the claim "Everyone thinks so," conjuring the image of a crowd huddling to confer on one's faults.

Those who find it hard to keep from repeating what they hear may be wise to decline to hear what they sense will put them in the difficult position of deciding whether or not to repeat it.

There are better and worse ways to deliver firsthand criticism as well. One type of no-fair criticism is to claim, "You *always* do this" instead of focusing on a specific instance of an action. Something one "always" does cannot be explained or even, often, envisioned. Furthermore, critics can try to restrict themselves to on-the-spot (in private) or brief-delay criticism. One who misses the chance to criticize at the time or soon after can rest assured that the behavior will recur. If it doesn't, then the criticism isn't needed. And reminding someone of something done wrong long ago compounds the hurt by implying the resentment has been harbored over time.

Advice to the Criticized

For the criticized, it helps to remember that criticism is a common by-product of closeness. It really is evidence of the presence, not the absence, of intimacy.

Beyond this, one should mount self-defense on the level of the pain—the effect of feeling criticized—rather than skirmishing about the validity of the criticism. When someone throws a ball at us, our reflex is to catch it. But with criticism, it is better to let the ball drop. Defending the way you did something invites a more elaborate explanation of why the critic thinks you did it wrong, and this is likely to trigger a bout of complementary schismogenesis. But if you say, "Constantly being told I'm doing things wrong makes me feel like a walking mistake," you are more likely to get an apology or at least a denial of intent to hurt. At the very least, it doesn't invite an escalation of criticism.

If speakers should avoid repeating criticism, hearers should protect themselves by cutting off reports of what others said about them before they are uttered. If they do hear it, they should bear in mind that what they hear is not the real truth but a version of it—and a distorted one at that.

Finally, the criticized can try not to overreact. Clearly Jake in Feiffer's *Grown Ups* had a damaging penchant for criticizing Louise, but he also had a point when he complained, "To you any criticism is a death blow." There are times when a partner needs to air legitimate complaints. Fearing to say anything at all critical is a little like feeling bound and gagged. It encourages the gunnysacking of unexpressed complaints.

Intimate criticism responds as well to a technique social scientists have used for years. On a recent visit, Jennifer's mother went to the closet, took out a broom, and began sweeping the kitchen floor. Jennifer felt the familiar rush of anger at being implicitly criticized. The indirectness of the slur on her housekeeping seemed not to mitigate but to aggravate it. But then Jennifer remembered her conversations with me and thought, "Oh, she's doing that again." Surprise! Jennifer's anger was gone. It had diminished as Jennifer drew back to become an observer rather than a player of the game.

Prevention and Cure

Continual criticism is a tragic failure of intimacy. From the craving to be close to someone and to feel accompanied through life is created not an ally but a close-up critic: someone on our own team ready to yell "Foul!" when a ball could easily have passed as within bounds; someone who has the dope on our past weaknesses to bring to bear on our present; someone looking at us so close up that our small blemishes appear, by a magnifying-glass effect, as monstrous in size.

The guidelines suggested for treatment of hard-core cases of intimate criticism are useful, but the proverbial prevention is worth more than the cure. We may not be able to obliterate the critical feeling, but we should be able to obliterate— indeed, *must* obliterate—the critical act. Calling upon the observer stance, we can register in our minds that Pat is doing that again—and keep our mouths shut.

IV.

What You Can and Can't Do with Conversational Style

CHAPTER TEN

Talking About Ways of Talking

Rachel regularly led training groups with a male colleague. He always did all the talking, and she was always angry at him for dominating and not giving her a chance to say anything. After hearing me talk about conversational style, she realized what was going on. He would begin to answer questions from the group while she was still waiting for a slight pause to begin answering. And when she was in the middle of talking, he would jump in—but always when she had paused. So she tried pushing herself to begin answering questions a little sooner than felt polite, and not to leave long pauses when she was talking. The result was that she talked a lot more, and the man was as pleased as she was. Her supervisor complimented her on having become more assertive.

Whether or not Rachel actually became more assertive is debatable. In a sense she did. What is crucial is that she solved her problem with a simple and slight adjustment of her way of speaking, without soul-searching, self-analysis, external intervention, and—most important—without defining herself as having an emotional problem or a personality defect: unassertiveness.

Humans want to understand their own and others' behavior. For humans in our society this often means seeking psychological explanations. If distress is extreme, they may seek psychological treatment. Plenty of situations and individuals warrant this. But before trying this drastic measure, it's a good idea to ask whether the problem may simply be differences in conversational style. If it is, it can be treated at home. If pain persists, see your doctor. But you may find that fewer visits to the doctor are really needed.

This book is not a self-help tricks-to-fix-it manual. Its main purpose is to shed light on human behavior, to offer understanding. The second part of this chapter shows how understanding in itself can go a long way toward solving problems. But, as Rachel's experience shows, knowledge of conversational style can be translated into steps to improve communication and, consequently, relationships. Many have been mentioned in previous chapters. They are briefly summarized in this one.

What to Do

The first step is to understand your own style: What are you doing when you communicate? What effect is it having on how others talk to you? How is your style a response to their way of talking to you? A way to help the process of observation is tape recording. With permission, of course, you can tape your conversations and listen to the tape to get a better understanding of how you and others talked and the effect this had on the interaction. If you aren't comfortable taping, or if the people you talk to aren't comfortable being taped, you can just observe.

As you get a sense of your own conversational style, there are ways you can adjust it. Here are some. You will doubtless think of others yourself.

If you expect people to continue talking over your listening talk, but you see that someone keeps stopping when you respond so that you seem to be interrupting, you can back off and listen more quietly. If you find yourself doing all the talking, you may try counting to six after you *think* the other person has finished or failed to take a turn, to make sure she isn't just gearing up to say something.

If you feel yourself being continually cut off, you may try to speed up, leaving smaller gaps between your turn and someone else's, and within your own talk. And you may force yourself not to stop when others start talking, but to talk right over them. If that doesn't work, you can try using a nonverbal sign of having something to say—like waving your hand or leaning forward.

Being aware of the danger of complementary schismogenesis—the spiraling effect of trying harder by applying more of the same style—you may resist the impulse to do more of the same and try doing something different. If you feel put off because someone is asking you too many questions, rather than evade the questions, you may try asking questions yourself, or pick a topic of interest to you and talk about it. From the other side, if you are asking questions to get someone talking, and he is answering in monosyllables or less, rather than asking more and different questions, you may stop asking them entirely and either volunteer information or let there be silence. No matter what the effect is, doing something different will at least change the interaction and stop the spiral of clashing styles.

Making More Friends

To illustrate how behaving differently can result in changing someone else's behavior, I will reproduce in its entirety an account—a story, really, but a true story—written by a young man who took my class in cross-cultural communication.

One Saturday morning, George, a friend of mine, and I were sitting at a table in the cafeteria for brunch. When we were almost done, Shawn, a friend of Paul's, came up and asked if she could join us. George said "of course" and introduced us to each other.

As soon as Shawn took her seat, she asked me where I came from. "China," I said. "Which one," she continued asking me. "Taiwan or the mainland?" "Mainland China," I answered.

"Oh, really? I have been to both Taiwan and Mainland China!" Then she started telling me all about her experiences in both Chinas. I was very interested in listening to her. From then on, she kept talking almost all the time without a break, giving us vivid narration of all sorts of interesting stories. As both George and I had already finished by this time, George had to excuse himself to leave. I, however, stayed on.

After another while, although I was interested in her chat, I remembered about my pile of homework that had to be done, so I said I had to leave too. She said she had also finished, so we walked out of the cafeteria together. All the while she was talking. By the time we had to separate, we stood there and she went on talking. Finally, when I realized that she had no intention of stopping, I apologized once again and said that I really had to go. We exchanged our telephone numbers and promised that we should get together sometime.

Not long after, again in the cafeteria, she suddenly showed up and took a seat in front of me when I was eating there alone. She started her chat right away. She had run out of things about China, and the topics now were very wide ranging. I can no longer remember all the contents of her talk.

We were eating together, and she was meanwhile talking all the time. When I needed to go to the serving area to get some more food, I was waiting for her to stop just for a second, so that I could have a chance to say, "Excuse me for just a minute." Unfortunately, she never stopped, not even for a second. Then I had an idea. I took up my plate and held it in my hand, to show her that I was really ready to go to get some more food, in the hope that she herself would offer to say: "Oh, you want some more food, you can go ahead." Same result. No feedback, and the chat went all the way on. Finally, I said, "I'll be back," and walked away, breaking her talk off rather rudely. However, she was very nice and did not take offense.

She was too nice. While I was standing in the line in the serving area, she came after me and went on talking. . . .

We ran into each other a couple of times after that. She wanted to talk, but I did not allow it, saying: "Sorry, I'm on my way to . . . I'm in a rush. . . ." She kept saying, "Call me, call me. We should get together sometime!" and I kept saying: "Yes, I will! Yes, I will!" She wanted to get together to show me something that I showed great interest to when we talked to each other at the first meeting. We finally agreed that we should plan to get together after the summer vacation started.

One evening during the first two weeks of the summer vacation, George called me up, saying that Shawn and he wanted to take me to an ice-cream place. I regretted that I could not make it, not because I did not want to talk to Shawn (although it was true at this time that I no longer felt comfortable to listen to her), but because I already had some other plans for the evening.

After that, I left the town for the summer. I came back to town right before this semester started. Although George and I had been in touch once in a while, I never heard another word about Shawn and I did not even bother to ask George about her.

Sometime in last month, October, I was surprised to run into Shawn and George together on campus again (both Shawn and George have graduated in this past May). At this time I was taking Dr. Deborah Tannen's course, Cross-cultural Communication, and had already realized to some extent about the problems between Shawn and me. So I took the chance to experience a different conversational style discussed by Dr. Tannen. After fair-weather talking, I initiated the conversation first by telling her all my experiences in Europe this past summer. She was very interested and related my experiences to her own in Europe. Whenever she cut me off, I immediately cut her off in return; whenever she raised her voice, I raised mine even higher. I tried by all means to dominate the conversation. She has a tendency of ignoring the third person present when she talks to someone. So, I cut her off many times to drag George into the conversation, to show that I controlled the conversation.

As a result, we got along extremely well this time. Once again I really had a lot of homework to do and I said at the start that I had to leave soon. But we turned out having stood in front of the library talking for three (!) hours. We had such a good time talking that we became oblivious to our surroundings. Both our voices were so high and loud, with my funny foreign accent on top of that, the people who have passed in front of the library several times already were curious if we were all right. A friend of George's asked him: "Hey, George! What's going on here?"

George and Shawn did take me out to a cafe the following week. Now Shawn and I are good friends, as we enjoy talking to each other. She has got a job in the area, and we talk quite regularly on the phone besides "getting together" once in a while!

From the first part of this story, the impression a reader gets is that Shawn is an intolerable person: a compulsive talker. But when the student changed his way of talking to her, her way of talking changed too. As a result he was able not only to tolerate her but to enjoy her company. He became friends with someone he would otherwise have fled from. As he himself commented, learning about conversational style enabled him to make more friends.

We tend to see our own behavior as a reaction to others; if we are rude to someone who has annoyed or offended us, we do not think this rudeness defines our personality; we think we were rude in that instance. But we think of others' personalities as absolute. If others are rude to us, we are likely to conclude that they are rude people, not that they are nice people who were rude in that instance—possibly in response to something we said or did If we realize that others' personalities and behavior are not absolute, we can see the possibility of changing them by changing our behavior toward them.

Metacommunicating and Reframing

The techniques mentioned thus far entail making small adjustments to conversational signals. This should be the first line of attack. But there are more drastic measures that can be taken, too.

As discussed in Chapter Five, a powerful tool is metacommunicating: talking about communication, with or without using the terms metamessage, frame, or conversational style. You may say something about what's going on—not, preferably, something judgmental like "Stop interrupting me" or "Give me a chance to talk," but something that focuses on your intentions, like "I want to say something but I need more time to get going" or "When I chime in, I don't expect you to stop. Go on." Another form of metacommunication is naming the frame: "I feel like we're having a shouting match. Can we slow it down?"

You may also ask the other person what she or he expected in response to a comment or question. You may be surprised by what you hear. For example, in the yogurt-dressing example in Chapter Eight, Ken was surprised to learn that Mike expected his question "What kind of salad dressing should I make?" to be thrown back on him: "Make whatever you like." And Mike was surprised to learn that Ken didn't expect him to make oil and vinegar dressing just because he answered, "Oil and vinegar, what else?" In addition, putting into words what you expected in response to what you said forces you to consider the other person's point of view.

The most powerful way to change interaction is to change the frame without making it explicit: reframing by talking or acting in a different way. Reframing is a repair job that often can be done most effectively behind the scenes.

The storeroom at a chemical laboratory was run by Mr. Beto, a non-native speaker of English. The director of the company received repeated complaints from chemists who had to get supplies from the storeroom; they said they could never get a straight answer from Mr. Beto. The director did not want to fire him because in every other way he was a capable, hardworking, and trustworthy employee.

Since the problem had to do with communication, the director assumed it was caused by Mr. Beto's lack of proficiency in speaking English. He decided to invest in English tutoring and called the head of the English As a Second Language Department at a nearby university who talked to Mr. Beto on the telephone and concluded that he spoke English well enough. She was certain that the problem was in Mr. Beto's interaction, not his language ability. She recommended me.

I had two meetings with Mr. Beto. At the first meeting he told me his view of his work situation, and I suggested he tape-record an on-the-job conversation. At the second meeting we listened to the tape. I could see immediately that he wasn't giving enough information to the chemist, who consequently had to question him (and did so with increasing impatience) in an attempt to find out what he needed to know. Mr. Beto also noticed that he was being asked a lot of questions, but he interpreted them differently. He said this was what he was up against—people were always grilling him because they doubted he knew what he was doing.

It was clear to me that complementary schismogenesis was

setting in. The more Mr. Beto felt that, through questioning, his competence and authority were being challenged, the more he evaded the questions, the more questions he was asked, and so on. Whereas the chemists were thinking of their questions simply for the message value—trying to get information—he was responding to the metamessage—questioning his competence.

I didn't try to explain any of this to Mr. Beto. Instead, I made a recommendation that proceeded from his assumptions. I suggested that he short-circuit people's attempts to undermine his position by volunteering in advance all the information they could possibly ask questions about. The result of this behavior would be exactly what the chemists wanted, without however endorsing their view or invalidating his. The director of the company later reported that the problem was solved: "People say he's speaking English now."

An interpretation of what was going on in this situation could have (correctly) entailed psychological analysis. But offering such analysis to Mr. Beto would have aggravated the situation by sending a metamessage that there was something wrong with him. And it would have taken a long time to get him to see the world in a new frame. English lessons, besides not confronting the problem, would also have been time consuming and expensive and would have reinforced the implication that Mr. Beto was lacking in competence. Intervening in terms of Mr. Beto's own frame was more efficient and bolstered rather than undermining his sense of control.

Let the Style Fit the Context

Work situations often require reframing because the strategies that have been learned and found to be effective in other contexts—among family and friends—may fail, partly because work is likely to bring us into contact with others whose styles differ, and partly because work situations may demand different self-presentation than social situations require. For example, beginning a discussion of where to go for dinner by starting a negotiation may be fine with some people in social settings. But trying to reach decisions by negotiation may be disastrous if you are a manager or a customer with a salesperson, because it may make you appear uncertain and open to pressure.

A manager interviewed an accountant for her company. The accountant stated that he would like a permanent arrangement working ten hours a week. The manager stated her budget limitations. Then they discussed the work that needed to be done. When she felt the interview had gone on long enough, the manager began to wrap it up by saying, "Well, what do you think we can arrange?" She expected not only to signal the beginning of the end of the meeting but also to initiate a negotiation so the accountant would feel he had participated in reaching an agreement. She expected the negotiation to go something like this:

Manager: Well, what do you think we can arrange?
Accountant: I'd like to work with you. What do you think you can offer?
Manager: I think I can get approval for about a thousand dollars' worth of consulting on this.
Accountant: That would be a start. For that amount, I can get your books in order and give you some pointers on how to keep them up.
Manager: That's reasonable. If that works out, we can see about where to go from there.

Instead, it went this way:

Manager: Well, what do you think we can arrange?
Accountant: Ten hours a week would be fine.

TILT! The interviewer's bid for a negotiation was taken by the accountant as an invitation to set his own terms. The manager was then in the position of having to deny his request, even more uncomfortable for her than single-handedly setting the terms in the first place. Although her style of negotiating would have worked well with some others, her role and the setting made it unwise to use a style that depended for its success on his having a congruent style. Framing the conversation as a negotiation was not effective here. Switching styles in this setting would reframe a conversation like this as "offering you a contract." Framing the interaction in this way, the manager would also appear—and be—more in control.

Use with Caution

Ironically, it is easier to make these changes and improve communication with others we don't know well and don't talk to frequently than it is with partners and family members. For one thing, it takes effort to convert processes that are normally automatic into conscious ones. Having to make this effort all the time, every day, can be exhausting.

Even more significant, your way of speaking is, in a sense, your identity. Talking differently makes one feel like a different sort of person. In a workshop I conducted on conversational style, a couple reported their own experience: They were taking out-of-town visitors to dinner; the husband was driving, and talking. As they drove past a building that the wife recognized as the one on the cover of the local telephone book, she tossed in a comment to that effect. The husband stopped talking and refused to go on, punishing her for interrupting. The wife said to him, "You heard what Dr. Tannen said. I'm just showing enthusiasm. Why don't you talk over me?" He responded, "I don't want to be a competitive talker." Even though he understood the mechanism of what was going on, he didn't want to change his way of talking because he didn't want to see himself as the sort of person who would talk that way.

Though he didn't accept her conclusion, this husband at least understood and accepted what his wife was talking about because he too had participated in the workshop. But someone who does not believe in metamessages, like Jake in Jules Feiffer's *Grown Ups*, won't know what you are talking about—or will claim not to know, with all the forces of conventional wisdom and "logic" on his side: After all, he didn't *say* that. This leaves you seeming to have a problem.

Some people, furthermore, persist in focusing on the aspects of speech they have always been aware of—accent, vocabulary, and rules of grammar—and cling to the conviction that their way of doing things is the right way. I encountered such a person in a well-known celebrity, when I was a guest on her talk show. I had been invited to discuss an article I had written about New York conversational style.

The host opened discussion by asking what makes the New York accent unique. After answering, I moved on to the subject of my article: New York conversational style. I talked at some length about overlap and interruption: Whereas some people feel certain that it is impolite to talk at the same time as someone else, there are many other people—many New Yorkers among them—for whom it is "polite" (that is, socially appropriate) to talk along with others as a way of showing enthusiasm, understanding, and rapport. For them, an overlap is not an interruption.

The host's response to my explanation was "That's because people don't learn to listen." When I said that my research proves that people can indeed talk and listen at the same time, she said, "It's just not polite. There are no manners considered here, are there?" In response to this, I offered a discourse on the relativity of concepts of politeness, in the course of which I began to say, "You may not think it's polite . . ." The host cut in at that point and said, "I don't. I absolutely don't," and soon moved on to ask, "But what is it about a New Yorker's vocabulary?"

Our conversation proceeded in this way. I never managed

to convince my host of the cultural relativity of politeness. At the end of the show, she thanked me for being her guest and told the listening audience, "If you talk like that—any of you—I'll be very angry!" And that was the last word.

Being on talk shows—especially call-in shows—is an excellent way to keep these limitations in perspective. In response to my discussion of conversational style, most callers enthusiastically thank me for casting light on issues that have caused them trouble and that they now feel they understand for the first time. But there are always a few who, like this celebrity host, continue to be convinced that there is an absolute sense of politeness, and theirs is it. A Texan who had the "aha!" response sent her mother a tape of a talk show on which I was a guest. After listening to the tape, the mother responded by reaffirming rather than reevaluating her negative feelings about Northerners. She wrote to her daughter: ". . . being from the North gives a very dominant viewpoint. . . . The South, West, and Southwest have completely different attitudes. The one thing that was never brought out [was that] the fact of not speaking out or interrupting is not so much culture as it is manners." The reason, of course, that this was not brought out in my interview is that it is precisely the misconception that I was trying to dispel! The point that was brought out (but didn't come through to this listener) was that manners are culture.

It is important, then, to be realistic in expectations of how others will respond to insights we offer. Whereas metacommunication—talking about communication—will be effective in some cases, it will not always be so. We cannot assume that we need only speak the truth to have others embrace it. Like the proverbial horse to water, some people who are led to the trough of the elixir of our version of truth will turn up their noses at it. Knowing about the relativity of conversational style is guaranteed to help; talking about it is often helpful but this is not guaranteed.

Another reason that metacommunication must be used with caution is that it puts the fact of communication problems on record, and, as explained in Chapter Seven, this in itself has a negative metamessage that we may want to avoid. It introduces a note of discord into interaction, along with the frame "working things out." If the other person is not someone you are very close to, talking about your relationship may frame it as closer than he wants it to be. If the relationship is a close one, as was shown in Chapter Seven, talking things out may have different meanings to each partner. While it may be a positive sign to one ("Our relationship is working because we can still work things out"), it may have a negative meaning to the other ("Our relationship is not working if we have to keep working it over").

Simply paying attention to the way others say things instead of to their intentions can annoy or anger them. Focusing on a level of meaning other than the one a speaker deems important is akin to the double-bind situation described by Gregory Bateson. He gave the example of a boy who raises a frog in his cupped hands. Taking a look, his mother says, "Your hands are dirty. Go wash them." This is insulting because the mother ignores what to the child was the point— the frog. It's maddening if he starts to wonder whether or not there ever was any frog, since his mother doesn't see it. This is what's maddening, too, about the proverbial "You're so cute when you're angry." It discounts the anger as a real message.

Talking about how someone spoke is a form of analysis, and some people resent being analyzed. They may feel that it frames them as the patient to your doctor. Remember Jake's challenge to Louise: "Is that another thing you know? My stare?" So sometimes even if you think you see what others are doing and why, you can't constructively tell them about it.

Knowledge Is Power

Because of these caveats, and despite the potential benefits of adjusting your style, metacommunicating, or reframing, the most significant outcome of knowing about conversational style is knowing itself: knowing that no one is crazy and no one is mean and that a certain amount of misinterpretation and adjustment is normal in communication.

To illustrate how knowledge itself can help, I quote from a letter articulating the sense of relief that comes from learning that what one has been criticized for is not crazy or bad but the logic of another system.

Dear Dr. Tannen,

I have just finished copy-editing your article [on New York Jewish conversational style] and, despite the fact that it is almost midnight and I've wanted since 9:30 to crawl into bed with a cup of tea and a book rather than do what I've been doing, I feel I must send you a thank you. . . .

I am not from New York (though I lived there for a while) but from Oregon and am not Jewish (though not much of anything else either). Your article nevertheless helps explain me to me and will, I hope, help to explain me to my husband who is inclined to tell me I talk too much and don't give other people a chance to finish what they want to say. (And having lived in Europe for the last eight years and, I assume, scaled down a bit, I tend to have the same reactions to some, though not all, Americans we meet.) It's been a source of all sorts of emotions for me—ranging from defensive rage to mea culpa breast-beating, and your article, though it doesn't furnish any "how-to" for adjusting to a quite different conversational environment, at least clues me in to some of the mechanisms at work.

Even with no suggestions for change at all, insight into the processes of conversational style brings relief in itself. As this reader explains, and as this book explains, if they don't know about conversational style, people look at the *results* of style differences and draw conclusions not about ways of talking but about personality and intentions. Drawing mistaken negative conclusions about, and having mistaken negative conclusions drawn by, strangers may be unpleasant; when it happens all the time (as in the case of this woman who lives abroad), it can have a cumulative effect of alternating anger at others and questioning of yourself. And when it happens with your living and loving partner, it can be deeply distressing—and mystifying. Understanding "some of the mechanisms at work" brings relief.

It is natural in interaction to assume that what you feel in reaction to others is what they wanted to make you feel. If you feel dominated, it's because someone is dominating you. If you can't find a way to get into a conversation, then someone is deliberately locking you out. Conversational style means that this may not be true. The most important lesson to be learned is not to jump to conclusions about others in terms of evaluations like "dominating" and "manipulative."

The Benefits of a Linguistic Approach

Everyone agrees that one of the biggest problems among people and nations is communication. We try to improve communication by talking things out, by being "honest." But if the problem is caused by differences in ways of talking, doing more of it is not likely to solve the problem. Honesty is not enough—and often not possible.

Most of us genuinely try to be honest and considerate and to communicate, but we sometimes end up in knots anyway, first, because communication is indirect and underdetermined by nature, and second, because of inevitable differences in conversational style. Seeing things go wrong, we look for explanations in personality, intentions, or other psychological motivations.

A psychotherapist who heard me talk at a Sunday evening lecture later told me that she put her new understanding of conversational style to use the very next morning. Her Monday-at-ten appointment arrived and began to talk. The therapist offered her interpretations and strategic questions as they were relevant. Each time, the client considered and discussed her comments, then returned to his account. He was a good patient. But her next client, Monday-at-eleven, was different. When she began making her comments (in other words, doing her job), he asked her not to interrupt. If she hadn't heard my talk, this therapist said, she would have concluded that Monday-at-eleven was resisting her interpretations. Recalling my lecture, however, she reserved judgment. Sure enough, after he finished what he had to say, he was just as eager to hear and consider her comments as Monday-at-ten. What was simply a style difference would have led her to unwarranted psychological evaluation.

Therapists, then, must consider the possibility of conversational-style differences before making psychological interpretations. And in personal rather than professional settings, it may be more effective to talk in terms of conversational style even when psychological motives are correctly observed.

Psychological motives are internal and amorphous; talk is external and concrete. If you tell others they were hostile or insecure, they may feel accused and may not know what you are reacting to. But if you say you reacted to how they said what they did, and you can pinpoint which aspect of the way they spoke you reacted to, they can see what was there and address it. If you begin by assuming that what you felt and what they intended are not necessarily the same, they are less likely to feel accused and to discount your reaction in self-defense.

Conversational style is normally invisible but not unconscious. People often say, spontaneously, "It's not what you said but the way you said it," even if they can't put their finger on just what it was about the way you said it that they reacted to. Knowing about conversational style gives names to what were previously felt as vague forces. Once pointed out, they have a ring of familiarity and truth.

A New Way of Talking—and Seeing

An idea that has been central to linguistics is the Sapir-Whorf Hypothesis, named for linguists Benjamin Lee Whorf and Edward Sapir. This is the idea that language shapes thought. We tend to think in the terms and related concepts our language gives us. It is easier to conceive of something if we have a word for it; we instinctively feel that something for which there is a word really exists. Anything for which there is no word seems somehow to lack substance. In this way, knowing the terms "frame," "metamessage," and "conversational style" makes it easier not only to talk about but also to think about how ways of talking shape communication.

People who enter psychotherapy or join a religious or human-potential movement soon begin to talk differently, using new words or, more common and more disconcerting to the uninitiate, using old words in new ways. It is inevitable and important for people who subscribe to a special way of thinking to develop a special way of talking also. For one thing, it establishes a feeling of a common point of view, of rapport, among those who share this way of talking—the "family joke" phenomenon. Also, perhaps most important, a new vocabulary and a new way of talking are tantamount to a new way of looking at the world.

Learning to talk about metamessages is also learning a new language and hence a new world view, but it doesn't (I hope) constitute a conversion in the religious sense, only a new focus of vision. Both science and art serve this function: helping people to see old things in new ways.

Power to the Metamessage

Having words for metamessages, frames, and conversational style gives credibility to them, more power to perceived but otherwise hard-to-defend emotions. People instinctively feel that their ways of expressing things and of being polite or rude are "natural" and "logical." Without the vocabulary and concepts presented here, these assumptions are hard to challenge.

Recall the experience of the husband who stopped talking because his wife interjected an unrelated comment. When first discussing the transcript of this conversation, participants in another workshop blamed the wife. A woman said "She's hostile!" A man said, "Her husband's talking and she just can't stand it. She has to stop him." This type of interpretation is especially common when the cooperative overlapper is female, because the image of an overbearing woman is a stereotypical and particularly fearsome one in our culture.

A person who needs time to finish what he is saying will justify this need by reference to logic: not that it is his style to avoid overlap, but that obviously no communication can take place if two people are talking at once. My research, and that of others, shows this to be untrue. It is possible, and common, in conversation for many people to be talking at once, and for everyone's ideas to get through eventually—*if* everyone understands the system, and no one rolls over and plays dead the moment someone else starts to vocalize. Rather, they all keep trying to say what they want until everyone is heard. (In fact, this all-together-now interaction-focused approach to conversation is more common throughout the world than our one-at-a-time information-focused approach.)

Being accused of rudeness or hostility hurts, especially if

we were intending just the opposite—friendliness. Here's another example of how this can happen, and how knowing about conversational style can help.

Vera was spending the Christmas holidays with her family. On Christmas day, she called Ed to let him know she was thinking of him. When he answered the phone, she bubbled, "Hi! How's it going?" Ed asked, in a frosty voice, "Who is this?"

Vera was cut to the quick but tried to be generous, figuring Ed must be in a bad mood. Yet actually he had been in an okay mood until Vera called. And it wasn't that he wasn't very fond of Vera. It was just that her starting to talk without identifying herself caught him off guard and seemed rude.

In Vera's style, identifying yourself by name on the phone is a formality reserved for relative strangers. With family members and close friends, skipping the formality sends a metamessage of rapport, following the rule of breaking rules. If someone is caught off guard, so much the better. The sudden frame switch is a source of amusement and delight. But Ed assumes self-identification is always a requirement, and he experiences no delight in being caught off guard.

Not knowing about conversational style, both Vera and Ed would find causes in personality: She's rude, he's moody, or intentions: He's trying to drive me away. And she would have no reason to act differently in the future; rather, she would try to nudge him out of his moodiness by being extra cheerful, greeting him in the same way, and—surprise!— "find" him in a bad mood again. By the process of complementary schismogenesis, both would get mounting evidence that the other is rude and moody. But knowing about conversational style, Ed and Vera were able to clarify that a style difference was sparking unfounded interpretations, and Vera realized that when calling Ed she should always say her name. Style switching saved the day.

Stepping Back

The key to solving this problem was the ability to step back and observe interaction rather than accepting emotional reactions as inevitable and unavoidable. This observer stance is what makes it possible to find one's own solutions and regain a sense of control over one's life and relationships. Another student explained how he developed the observer stance as a result of taking my class:

> What I found to be the strangest thing of all was being conscious of doing all these things that are normally not conscious behavior. . . . Every time I would do something like this, I would stop myself and wonder: Why did I do that? or What am I doing this for? It is kind of strange, peering into one's motives and supposedly unconscious behavior, and trying to explain them. . . . The key, it seems to me, is simply to be <u>more aware</u> of what is going on and <u>not biased</u> by my own cultural predispositions and expectations. . . . To the extent that [the course] opened me up to all this new knowledge . . . [it has] been invaluable in helping me to understand what is going on around me.

The observer stance is particularly useful if you find yourself in a situation you don't like. You can save the occasion by becoming an observer—trying to figure out what it is about the situation that you are reacting to, possibly thinking of ways you could prevent it from happening in the future. A motto might be: If you can't fight it, study it.

Stepping back and analyzing an interaction is a good antidote to overinvolvement. This is what happened when Kate (as reported in Chapter Nine) saw her mother's apparent criticism as part of a recognizable pattern of behavior ("Oh, my mother's doing that again") and her anger dissolved. Nothing had changed, but she acquired emotional distance by becoming an observer.

Widening the Lens

The processes of conversational style that play themselves out in private conversations are also at the heart of public and international relations. Conversational style has something to say to all the situations in which people talk to each other: in business, in court, in doctors' offices. It has something to say to the issue of social justice.

One of the great puzzles and tragedies of our time is that affirmative action has not worked as well as expected. Affirmative action programs were designed to ensure access for people from those groups who had previously not had access. But people of different backgrounds tend to behave and talk in different ways—ways that are incomprehensible to, incompatible with, or simply misunderstood by those who are already in mainstream organizations. That's why so many Americans have been shocked to discover racial, ethnic, or gender-based prejudice in themselves—and why discrimination remains such an incalcitrant problem in our (truly, I believe) well-intentioned society.

Just like lovers or spouses blaming each other for miscommunication, individuals in cross-cultural contact tend to blame the other group. "Mainstream" or "establishment" types blame the newcomers for not behaving right once they're let in. Members of less privileged groups—blacks, Jews, women, and so on—find it easy and obvious to attribute their treatment to the army of isms: racism, anti-Semitism, sexism. Surely there do exist some nasty ists who believe and practice these various isms. But not enough to account for the situation. Most Americans genuinely believe that everyone should be given equal opportunity. But they balk, in confusion, disillusionment, and dismay, when culturally different people, having been optimistically admitted, do not behave in expected (and they think self-evidently appropriate) ways.

If social justice is a gnawing problem within our country, the problem of international relations is a gnawing problem in the world. Often ill will among nations is exacerbated if not caused by differences in ways of showing intentions. An Egyptian living in the United States was surprised and hurt to learn that his American roommate considered Egyptian President Anwar Sadat to be "rude and arrogant." The American was responding to Sadat's comment, in answer to an American journalist's question: "Invited or not invited, I will come" to discuss peace negotiations with President Carter. The Egyptian immediately recognized his president's statement as an English translation of a standard formulaic expression that Egyptians commonly use to show the very best intentions to settle a misunderstanding and restore harmonious relations.

In the arena of world affairs, misunderstandings can have literally fatal consequences. A sociolinguist gave the example of an Egyptian pilot who radioed ahead to the Cyprus airport for permission to land. Receiving no reply, the pilot took silence to mean assent: permission granted. As he brought his plane in for a landing, the Cypriot air force opened fire on it. To the air-traffic controllers, silence obviously meant "permission denied."

Misunderstandings are not always so easily glossed. International relations are largely a matter of individuals sitting down and talking to each other, and are therefore subject to misunderstandings and bad feelings due to missed timing, incongruent rhythms, all the subtle differences in ways of talking that can lead to negative conclusions—and are even more serious and more inevitable in communication among people who speak different languages and come from different countries. But if we don't find ways of improving communication in these settings, nuclear war may end our problems at home.

The public tragedies of social discord and injustice, and the failure to reach international understanding, are large-scale manifestations of the failure of communication that plays itself out in private homes. People are genuinely surprised and disappointed when their good will doesn't ensure mutual understanding. It is the hope of this book that insight into conversational style will enhance if not ensure mutual understanding.

Notes

CHAPTER ONE:
The Problem Is the Process (pp. 17–28)

p. 20. Bettelheim writes in *The Informed Heart* that people can put up with almost anything if they can see the reason for it.

CHAPTER TWO:
The Workings of Conversational Style (pp. 29–44)

p. 31. The terms *metamessage* and *double bind* are found in G. Bateson (1972). For Bateson, a double bind entailed contradictory orders at different levels: the message and metamessage conflict. I use the term, as do other linguists (for example, Scollon 1982), simply to describe the state of receiving contradictory orders without being able to step out of the situation.

p. 31. I am grateful to Pamela Gerloff for bringing to my attention Bettelheim's (1979) reference to Schopenhauer's porcupine metaphor.

p. 34. M. C. Bateson (1984) discusses G. Bateson's idea that living systems (biological processes as well as human interaction) never achieve a static state of balance, but achieve balance only as a series of adjustments within a range.

p. 34. For his conversational maxims see Grice (1975).

p. 35. Lakoff's original statement of the rules of politeness is in Lakoff 1973. She also presents this system in the context of discussing male/female differences (Lakoff 1975). A more recent article describes the system as a continuum (Lakoff 1979). Brown and Levinson (1978) provide an extended and formalized discussion of politeness phenomena.

p. 41. Kochman (1981) presents an extended analysis of *Black and White Styles in Conflict*.

p. 43. The quotation from *Annie Hall* is taken from the screenplay by Woody Allen and Marshall Brickman in *Four Films of Woody Allen* (NY: Random House, 1982).

CHAPTER THREE:
Conversational Signals and Devices (pp. 45–62)

p. 48. Understanding conversation as a matter of signaling how one means what one says by use of conversational signals is based on the work of Gumperz (1982), who calls these signals "contextualization cues." The constellation of signals laid out here, and the notion of their being used to make up conversational devices, is mine. My research on conversational analysis is presented in more detail and placed in theoretical context in Tannen (1984).

CHAPTER FOUR:
Why We Don't Say What We Mean (pp. 65–81)

p. 65. Uses of indirectness are discussed by Lakoff (1973, 1975, 1979).

CHAPTER FIVE:
Framing and Reframing (pp. 82–100)

p. 82. Framing and metacommunication are introduced in Bateson (1972). A lot has been written about frames in linguistics, anthropology, psychology, and artificial intelligence. For a start, see Tannen (1979), Goffman (1974), and papers collected in Raskin (1985).

p. 86. The question of the impossibility of having a verbatim transcript, and the impact of punctuation on the impression made by a transcript of a legal proceeding, are the subjects of a doctoral dissertation by Walker (1985).

p. 88. Raskin (1984) analyzes jokes as frame switches.

p. 99. The idea that communication is a continuous stream, which can be interpreted differently depending on where it is punctuated, is also developed by Bateson (1972).

CHAPTER SIX:
Power and Solidarity (pp. 101–117)

p. 101. The dimension of power and solidarity is among the bedrock concepts of sociolinguistics. Brown and Gilman (1960) introduced the concept and used pronouns to illustrate it.

p. 105. Erving Goffman led me to see the predicament of the man who called the executive "honey." I had told the story in conversation, aware only of the offense involved. Goffman pointed out to me that the language as we know it provided the man no means of being friendly to a woman in the way that he could have been to a man, without offending.

p. 113. The analysis of the conversation among Ben, Ethel, and Max is in Sacks (1971). I am grateful to Jim Schenkein, who taped the conversation, for giving me permission to reproduce it here, and to Emanuel Schegloff for granting permission to recap Sacks's analysis of it. Sacks notes in his lecture that, whereas he and other professional conversational analysts normally labored over transcripts to represent every pause and pronunciation exactly right, the transcript of this conversation is a rough one. For that reason I took the liberty of making a few small changes in punctuation in order to make it easier to read.

CHAPTER SEVEN:
Why Things Get Worse (pp. 121–132)

p. 124. The article on summit conferences appeared in *Newsweek*, May 30, 1983.

p. 129. Bateson (1972) introduces the term complementary schismogenesis. M. C. Bateson (1984) discusses it and notes that her father later subsumed it under "regenerative feedback." (The excerpt quoted here comes from this book, p. 96.)

CHAPTER EIGHT:
Talk in the Intimate Relationship:
His and Hers (pp. 133–151)

p. 133. I always feel uneasy when I talk about male/female differences. There are many for whom the suggestion that there are such differences constitutes ideological heresy, and there are others who maintain that even if such differences exist, it is best not to talk about them, because anything that bolsters the idea that women are different from men will be used to denigrate women. (The same can be said of research on racial, ethnic, and class differences.) I see this danger, and I also see the danger of generalizing, especially when not enough research has been done to test intuition and observation. There are always exceptions to general patterns, and describing the patterns seems to slight the individuals who are exceptions. (To such individuals I offer sincere apologies.) But I decided to go ahead and confront these issues because I have found that talking about male/female differences in this way evokes a very strong "aha" response: Many people exclaim that this description fits their experience and that seeing what they previously perceived as their individual problem in terms of a widespread pattern lifts from them a burden of pathology and isolation. Questions will doubtless remain about the generalizability of my observations and the cultural versus biological sources of differences. If the result is to spark questioning and observation by both researchers and individuals in their lives, it will be all to the good.

p. 141. Hacker makes this point in "Divorce à la Mode," *The New York Review of Books*, May 3, 1979, p. 24.

p. 142. Information in the section "Growing Up Male and Female" is based on Maltz and Borker (1982).

CHAPTER NINE:
The Intimate Critic (pp. 152–173)

p. 158. The story by Charles Dickinson, "Sofa Art," appeared in *The New Yorker*, May 6, 1985.

CHAPTER TEN:
Talking About Ways of Talking (pp. 177–200)

p. 199. The example of Sadat's use of a formulaic expression is in a dissertation proposal by Hassan Hassan, Georgetown University Linguistics Department.

p. 199. The example of the Egyptian pilot is in Saville-Troike (1985).

Bibliography

Bateson, Gregory. 1972. *Steps to an Ecology of Mind*. New York: Ballantine.

Bateson, Mary Catherine. 1984. *With a Daughter's Eye: A Memoir of Margaret Mead and Gregory Bateson*. New York: William Morrow.

Bettelheim, Bruno. 1979. *Surviving*. New York: Knopf.

Brown, Roger, and Albert Gilman. 1960. "The Pronouns of Power and Solidarity." In Thomas Sebeok, ed., *Style in Language*. Cambridge, Mass.: The MIT Press, pp. 253–276.

Brown, Penelope, and Stephen Levinson. 1978. "Universals in Language Usage: Politeness Phenomena." In Esther Goody, ed., *Questions and Politeness*. Cambridge, England: Cambridge University Press, pp. 56–289.

Goffman, Erving. 1974. *Frame Analysis*. New York: Harper and Row.

Grice, H. P. 1967. "Logic and Conversation." William James Lectures, Harvard University. Reprinted in Peter Cole and Jerry Morgan, eds., *Syntax and Semantics, Vol. 3: Speech Acts*. New York: Academic Press, 1975.

Gumperz, John J. 1982. *Discourse Strategies*. Cambridge, England: Cambridge University Press.

Kochman, Thomas. 1981. *Black and White Styles in Conflict*. Chicago: University of Chicago Press.

Lakoff, Robin. 1973. "The Logic of Politeness, or Minding Your P's and Q's. Papers from the Ninth Regional Meeting of the Chicago Linguistics Society, pp. 292–305.

Lakoff, Robin. 1975. *Language and Woman's Place*. New York: Harper and Row.

Lakoff, Robin Tolmach. 1979. "Stylistic Strategies Within a Grammar of Style." In Judith Orasanu, Mariam K. Slater, and Leonore Loeb Adler, eds., *Language, Sex, and Gender*. Annals of the New York Academy of Science, Vol. 327, pp. 53–78.

Maltz, Daniel N., and Ruth A. Borker. 1982. "A Cultural Approach to Male-Female Miscommunication." In John J. Gumperz, ed., *Language and Social Identity*. Cambridge, England: Cambridge University Press, pp. 196–216.

Raskin, Victor. 1984. *Semantic Mechanisms of Humor*. Dordrecht, Holland, and Boston: D. Reidel.

Raskin, Victor, ed. 1985. *The Quaderni di Semantica's Round Table Discussion of Frame Semantics*. Special issue of *Quaderni di Semantica*, Vol. 6, No. 2.

Sacks, Harvey. 1971. Lecture notes, March 11, 1971.

Saville-Troike, Muriel. 1985. "The Place of Silence in an Integrated Theory of Communication." In Deborah Tannen and Muriel Saville-Troike, eds., *Perspectives on Silence*. Norwood, N.J.: Ablex.

Scollon, Ron. 1982. "The Rhythmic Integration of Ordinary Talk." In Deborah Tannen, ed., *Analyzing Discourse: Text and Talk*. Georgetown University Round Table on Languages and Linguistics 1981. Washington, D.C.: Georgetown University Press, pp. 335–349.

Tannen, Deborah. 1979. "What's in a Frame? Surface Evidence for Underlying Expectations." In Roy O. Freedle, ed., *New Directions in Discourse Processing*. Norwood, N.J.: Ablex, pp. 137–181.

Tannen, Deborah. 1984. *Conversational Style: Analyzing Talk Among Friends*. Norwood, N.J.: Ablex.

Walker, Anne. 1985. *From Oral to Written: The "Verbatim" Transcription of Legal Proceedings*. Ph.D. dissertation, Georgetown University.

Index

BOOKS BY
DEBORAH TANNEN

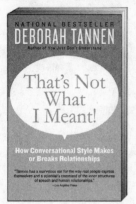

THAT'S NOT WHAT I MEANT!
How Conversational Style
Makes or Breaks Relationships

ISBN 978-0-06-206299-4 (paperback)

A reissue of the classic bestseller offering
Deborah Tannen's entertaining, informative, and
original linguistic approach to understanding the
powerful role of conversational signals and style
in relationships of any kind.

YOU JUST DON'T UNDERSTAND
Women and Men in Conversation

ISBN 978-0-06-095962-3 (paperback)

Deborah Tannen's fascinating book explores in depth
the different conversational styles between men and
women by offering clear analyses of conversational
exchanges between the sexes, excerpts from the works
of linguists, and samples from various media including
TV and novels.

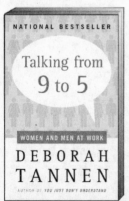

TALKING FROM 9 TO 5
Women and Men at Work

ISBN 978-0-380-71783-5 (paperback)

Bestselling author Deborah Tannen brilliantly explains
women's and men's conversational rituals in this unique
and invaluable guide to recognizing the verbal power
games and miscommunications that cause good work to
be underappreciated or go unnoticed.